'The research that went into the book was obviously meticulous and painstaking, but equally obviously it was a labour of love.'
THE IRISH TIMES

Old Days, Old Ways

Olive Sharkey is the daughter of farmers in the midlands of Ireland. 'I belong to a family which was the last in our district to relinquish the old ways on the land and in the home,' she says. Her research brought her to folk museums throughout Ireland and 'into the homes of fascinating elderly folk with surprisingly clear memories.'
The daily and seasonal rhythms of life and work 'in the ould days' is recaptured, from building the house and turning the sod for a new crop, to saving the hay and burying the dead.

⎯⎯⎯⎯⎯⎯

Olive Sharkey has worked as an architect's draftsperson, and after her marriage she began writing and drawing and contributing to newspapers and magazines. Her other interests include natural history and photography.

Timothy P. O'Neill, author of *Life and Traditions in Rural Ireland* and for eight years affiliated with the Folk Life Section of the National Museum of Ireland, teaches history at the Carysfort College of Education.

Old Days
Old Ways

Text and Illustrations

OLIVE SHARKEY

Foreword

TIMOTHY P. O'NEILL

THE O'BRIEN PRESS

First published 1985 by The O'Brien Press Ltd.,
20 Victoria Road, Rathgar, Dublin 6, Ireland
Reprinted 1987, 1991, and 1994

British Library Cataloguing-in-publication Data
Sharkey, Olive
Old days old ways: an illustrated folk
history of Ireland.
I. Ireland - History
1. Title
941.5 DA910

ISBN 0-86278-258-9

10 9 8 7 6 5 4

Book and cover design: Michael O'Brien
Cover illustration: Marie Hanlon
Editing: Íde ní Laoghaire
Typesetting: Phototype-Set Ltd.
Printing: Colour Books, Dublin

Contents

For my father
Patrick Donegan
the inspiration behind this book

Foreword

'There were good times once, not your time or my time but somebody's time . . . .' This saying from the midlands of Ireland was often used to begin a story and it sprang to mind as I read this book for the first time. Like the author I enjoyed a youth in that area and these pages brought back those days to me. Her descriptions of reaping and threshing machines brought to mind the whole hurly burly of those activities. Her descriptions of quieter moments of rural life are also here. Reading these pages I experienced something of the comfort of those old days, and it is impossible not to feel nostalgic about those times which are no longer my time or your time but are still perhaps somebody's time.

The author draws on her own experience and on her searches in published work and museums for her sources. It is when she writes from her own experience that she is most impressive. She knows and loves the artifacts she describes. She writes beautifully about the charge of feeling that is implicit in objects that have been handled over the generations – things like forks and spades, bowls and dishes, hearths and houses.

The book is located in the midlands, that part of Ireland which covers perhaps half a dozen counties and which forms a kind of cultural zone distinguishable mainly because of what it is not. It is not the gaelic zone of the west, it is not the anglicised east, it is not the north with its Scottish cultural implants, and it lacks the cultural definition so easily recognised in the southern counties. The midlands are, and have been, a cultural frontier zone borrowing from all sides of the divide. In this area the remains of the material culture, like the folklore and customs of the area, are rich in their diversity. While social reformers changed the west and prosperity and cultural innovation affected the east, the midlands remained the forgotten region where people never starved, rarely became millionaires but retained a steadier lifestyle which is often the most favourable condition for the survival of old ways and old things. This is the author's unique region. Much of the material described here is anachronistic because of the pace of change of modern life, even in the midlands, since the 1960s. It will be the challenge to the next generation to chart how the area adapted change to local ways and to see how the old ways were affected by the new innovations. Material culture is an important part of the cultural history of any country. It has a real and fundamental contribution to make to local history studies in showing in the round the way of life and economy of an area, and the course of change and development over time. Olive Sharkey's work is a welcome addition to the growing literature in this field.

A glance at the table of contents will show the wide range of topics this book examines. There is a growing archive of published material in this field both from academic writers and from local enthusiasts like Olive Sharkey. To each topic discussed she brings an easy familiarity, an understanding and insight which comes from a closeness to her subject. To what will be the undoubted fury of those who would prefer a more academic approach she refers to the objects she describes as 'bygones', but her approach has the advantage of being both a generalised approach and a recording of one person's memories. Hers is a personal record of the bygones of her experience to which she has added her discoveries in a wider search for information. All of this she presents in an easy conversational tone. In every chapter her reminiscences make the subject matter personal. This is indeed a rich garnering of stuff which must inevitably command the attention of the scholar.

This book is copiously illustrated. The author's line drawings are clear and clean and the subject matter is varied. The author has been diligent in searching out her material. It is unusual to find a midland author showing this interest. It is to be hoped that the national collection of folklife objects stored in the old reformatory in Daingan, County Offaly, will soon be put into a proper museum so that many others may join the author in her enthusiasm for these old objects.

Reading this book was for me a *recherche du temps perdu*, a discovery and as often a recovery of times past. I look forward to other books from this author.

Dublin, February 1987   *Timothy P. O'Neill, Ph.D.*

Introduction

When compiling this book I never intended to produce a study of Irish folk history or a detailed analysis of our recent past, but rather a compendium of old bygones. A lot of research was necessary, taking me into the musty and often cobwebby depths of folk museums where I became more and more intrigued with the range of bygones in the various exhibitions, and into the homes of fascinating elderly folk with surprisingly clear memories. My father, to whom I dedicate this book, was a mine of information and nostalgia about my own ancestral history, regaling me with yarns about life 'in the ould days'.

Many great writers and historians have expounded at length on the subject of Irish folk history in virtual tomes of information, but very few have contributed more than a few illustrations. It was this fact that first got me thinking about the possibility of compiling a book of old bygones – the tools, vessels and gadgets in everyday use when our parents and grandparents were children. Also, I belong to a family which was the last in our district to relinquish the old ways on the land and in the home. I have clear memories – happy memories – of seeing my father doing his farmwork with semi-primitive machines, of Dolly, the workhorse, and of seeing my mother churning the old way and fetching the water from the local pump in metal cans. It was a hard enough existence for them, but at least they had the comforts of a new, bright and airy home and electricity. My grandparents and their contemporaries didn't, at least not until they were too old to benefit from the improvements, so their lives must have seen a lot of hardship and drudgery. I wanted to document this as well to some degree.

Bygones tell their own story of how it must have been. I look at an old black kettle and am immediately transported back to a dark kitchen smelling of freshly baked bread and of turf-smoke with the solemn tick of a clock beating a slow tattoo in the background; and the sight of an old rusty plough reminds me of the smell of earth and the raucous whimpering of gulls rising and dipping behind my father as he slowly guided the horse and plough in other times. Other bygones, however, failed to inspire such thoughts simply because they were alien to me prior to researching this book, but perhaps they will evoke pleasant memories for others.

My research brought me to countryside museums in England and Scotland as well as Ireland. I found a lot of similarities between folk life in Britain and folk life in Ireland, and, equally, a lot of interesting contrasts. Our social history made for different needs amongst the peasants, and our climate and terrain for a different type of vernacular architecture.

Our folk history is intrinsically ours and the bygones I've accumulated in this book are a very important part of that history and should not be ignored. I hope that by cataloguing them in this way I've helped to ensure their survival in our memories.

Olive Sharkey

Chapter 1

The Thatched House

The traditional Irish thatched house is perhaps one of the most appealing and most evocative sights the modern-day traveller in Ireland will meet. Yet, we must go deep into the hinterland before we encounter such a sight, and even then it will be less than authentic, for most thatched houses today play host to a whole gamut of anachronisms, such as furniture which rightfully belongs in what used to be called the 'big house', and electricity, which undoubtedly enhances the life of the modern house dweller, but doesn't – strictly speaking – belong.

The thatched house is virtually extinct as a 'natural' feature of the Irish countryside. For two reasons: firstly, modern house buyers want modern homes with modern amenities, and secondly, thatched houses are surprisingly expensive to maintain. For one thing, the cost of employing a thatcher to service the roof on a fairly regular basis is colossal. In the past good thatchers were two-a-penny in the rural areas, but nowadays one would have to travel a long way to find a skilled thatcher, especially one who is prepared to exercise his talents in all weathers.

The history of the thatched house as we know it doesn't go back as far as one might expect. Such houses began to be built probably at the end of the seventeenth century. It is generally believed that many of these early homes were erected within settlements now referred to as *clacháns,* a few of which survive today in isolated, underdeveloped parts of the country. Basically, a *clachán* was a small cluster of houses in a farming community, and the farmers worked the land surrounding the *clachán.*

During the eighteenth century the small farmers of Ireland were experiencing relative peace, but small outbreaks of famine and stress due to crop failure occurred with ominous regularity, culminating in the Great Famine of the 1840s. We are all well aware of the strife and misery the Famine brought in its wake, and the serious setback it caused to what little development was being made in rural areas. It took the survivors a long time to get back on the road to improvement again.

By the early twentieth century, when my own grandparents were setting up home, virtually all farmhouses were rectangular in shape and were built with great attention to detail and even a small degree of flair, and finished off with a neat canopy of thatch which looked particularly beautiful when it was first put on and still a lovely shade of burnished gold. Much pride was being taken in the general appearance of the home, both inside and out, and geraniums in big black three-legged pots held court outside many a front door, and sprawling creepers clung to the front walls just as they did to the front walls of the 'big house'.

I have some fond memories of my grandparents' house, and of childhood days spent virtually under my poor granny's feet. My memories are twofold: of the happy days when the house was a home and my granny was in residence, and the sadder days when the house was being razed to the ground soon after she died. I can still see in my mind's eye the great, thick external walls as my father brought them slowly to the ground, using just a pick, a shovel and a big iron bar. And I can remember the acrid smell of the rotten thatch.

BUILDING THE THATCHED HOUSE

When a new house was being constructed in those days they didn't have to wait for planning permission or any other bureaucratic nonsense! They would simply choose a site, and a few friends would volunteer their help for a couple of months, the time it took to erect the house. The whole exciting business would then be the main topic of conversation and speculation for miles around.

To the casual observer the traditional Irish houses all look alike, but a close examination will reveal not only superficial differences, such as different thatch finishes, but also structural differences not apparent until the buildings are being knocked down, and differences in the layout of certain features within the buildings. Some houses, for instance, had bed alcoves incorporated, others had a dairy built onto one end, and so on.

Some early thatched houses were built on virtually no foundation at all, but most of those constructed since the early 1800s had strong

---

Figure 1 A: chimneyless pre-Famine stone cabin; B: stone chimney; C: wooden chimney; D: wattle-and-daub chimney-breast of ruined 18th c. cottage; E: bogman's peat cabin and plan; F: pre-Famine peat cabin, commonly built in north west; G: external wall of ruined coastal cottage, showing projecting pegs for roof ropes.

A

B

C

D

E

plan

B.

F

G

Fig 1

stone foundations. The trenches were dug out by hand to a depth of up to two feet and filled in with stones and mortar or clay to bind them. The hearth wall was continued up to roof level in stone, and sometimes even the external walls were constructed from stone, or a mixture of stones and mortar. Clay figured strongly in the midlands where it was easily acquired, and usually the internal partition walls were built from a mixture of muddy clay and wattles, a mixture known as wattle-and-daub. Clay was sometimes used in the construction of the floor too, although flagstone floors were more popular, especially in farmhouses, because they were easier to clean. However, a besom or broom could remove the top stratum of clay from a clay floor in just one sweep.

Roof frames differed considerably from region to region, with less perceptible differences within districts. Bog oak was used in the construction of the rafters, being both strong and durable. The coupled roof was widely used and this is how E. E. Evans describes it, in relation to houses in the north of Ireland, in *Irish Folk Ways* (London, 1957): 'The coupled rafters are joined by one or two cross-ties secured by wooden pins, and pegs driven into the rafters hold in place the long purlins which support a layer of branches or thin laths of bog-fir. On these rests a warm blanket of carefully fitted sods (scraws), an essential element in the traditional roof, keeping out cold and damp and serving as a hold for the rods (scollops) with which the thatch, over the greater part of the country is secured.' The practice of insulating with sods was followed also in the midlands, although not in other parts of the country. Such insulation ensured that the house was warm and snug during the icy months of winter and remarkably cool in summer. I have often heard my father say that the thatched house was the coolest place to be on a warm summer's day.

The features of the house, such as windows, doors, and so on, were determined not only by personal preference on the part of the owner, but also by tradition and by necessity. Window openings, for instance, were always very small and few in number, a tradition born of necessity. Prior to 1800 window taxes were levied on the number and sizes of windows, and those who couldn't see their way to paying very much made sure they allowed only the minimum amount of daylight and fresh air into the home. Consequently they might develop typhus due to lack of fresh air, and deaths from this disease

---

Figure 2 A: single-roomed stone cabins, *c.* 1800; B: stone farmhouse with attic space utilised by humans whilst animals occupied ground floor; C: coastal house with roped thatch; D: two-roomed house, once common in the Meath area in 1800s; E: two-roomed house with hearth at each end, with plan above; F: Donegal 'longhouse' and plan.

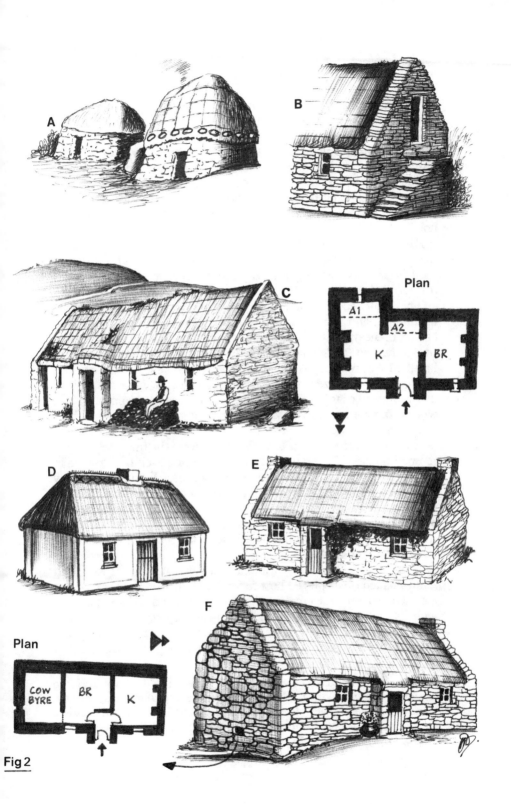

A

B

C

Plan

A1
A2
K   BR

D

E

F

Plan

COW
BYRE   BR   K

Fig 2

were not unknown. The tax became known as the typhus tax as a result.

The traditional half-door was a common feature in some areas, yet was unknown in others. Its advantages were important, especially where the windows admitted little light or air. It allowed a good deal of both daylight and fresh air to filter into the house, whilst at the same time keeping hungry hens out and crawling babies in. It also served as an arm-rest for the farmer while he smoked his 'baccy' and chatted to a passing neighbour. And when he was inside, seated by the fire, it afforded him a fine view of visitors as they approached the house.

All thatched houses, with the exception of some of the thatched mansions, were a single room in width, and anyone who added to their home by extending it in any other direction was doomed to a future filled with bad luck!

The thatched mansion was the forerunner of the Georgian farmhouse, and was invariably the property of the local 'big-shot' farmer in the district. There was just such a house in our townland, a fine rambling old house which was abandoned for a modern farmhouse as recently as twenty-five years ago or so. It was spacious inside, with a dozen fine rooms, including a rather primitive bathroom and a larder. An imposing facade suggested a mansion but, when examined from the side, the building showed itself to be a single room in width.

And at the other end of the scale there were the tiny one- or two-roomed houses. The poorest of these were the hovels constructed in the bogs by the turf-cutters for their own use. Fashioned crudely from sods of turf and roofed with a covering of heathery thatch, they just about kept the winds at bay. On very cold nights a pole with a bundle of hay tied to it was drawn into the narrow doorway; rarely was there anything resembling a window, and if a chimney existed it was only a hole in the roof.

A turf-cutter invariably fashioned his own new home from bog scraws which often played host to families of pissmires (a sort of bog ant). These busy little creatures had no qualms about sharing a hovel with its builder, which was fine so long as they kept a safe distance from each other! When they came in close contact, the pissmire showed displeasure by emitting a strong stinging acid which didn't

---

Figure 3 A: inland cottage, midlands; B: woven rush door, used prior to advent of wooden doors; C: thatched farmhouse from south east, once the home of Edmund Ignatius Rice (see also plan on left); D: thatched mansion; E: battering ram poised for eviction in penal times; F: cottage with bed alcove; G: interior view of bed alcove.

A

B

Plan ►►

C

D

E

F

G

Fig 3

exactly endear it to the turf-cutter. However, the turf-cutter was a quiet man and probably accepted the pissmire as an occupational hazard.

Another type of thatched house, sometimes found in Donegal and often referred to as the Donegal longhouse, was a stone building built on a slope, with the slope built into the floor as well. The building housed man and beast together, and the slope was concentrated in the lower end of the two-roomed building, the part occupied by the animals. The family lived in the same room and slept in a second compartment beyond the hearth. The cows and other animals spent the winter in the house, enjoying the heat from the open hearth and a warm bed of straw, while the humans chatted not ten feet from them.

Drainage in this kind of house was not a problem. Sunken floor channels, sloping away from the centre of animal occupation, provided adequate drainage, while external channels took the waste matter from the wall of the house to a pit a good distance away, usually alongside the dungheap in the yard. This custom of housing man and beast together is believed to go right back to prehistoric times, with the most recent example of this particular housing arrangement visible on the island of Inisbofin.

THE THATCHER (TUÍODÓIR)

The rural thatcher was an important craftsman; his services were required at all times of the year, not alone for roof thatching, but also for rick thatching, which was important in the wealthier farming communities. The craft of the thatcher was one which 'many men could do, but few could do well', and it often took a thatcher many years of trial and error to accomplish a skill of which he could be proud.

The thatcher was his own master, hardy, tough and independent, with no two operating in exactly the same way. Sometimes their work could be recognised individually, some displaying simple techniques and plain sensible work, others displaying ostentation and clever but painstakingly accomplished gimmickry. During heavy rains and other bad spells of weather when the thatcher couldn't work on the roof, he spent his time usefully making scollops (*scolbacha*). These were also known as rods or spars, and the slightly longer ones as sways. In some areas scollop-making was an important local

Figure 4   A: coastal farmhouse; B: the half-door; C: detail of wattle-and-daub interior wall; D: structural details of walls (midlands) – a = sods, b = wattle-and-daub, c = stone; E: coupled rafters on ruined house; F: stone gable with rope-pegs; G: plastered gable with stone rope-pegs; H: internal view of coupled rafters.

Fig 4

industry, the sole concern of one man who worked in liaison with all the local thatchers, and in those days there was one in nearly every townland. However, some thatchers liked to work independently, cultivating their own sally or hazel coppice. Essentially the scollop was a twisted length of sally (hazel in the midlands), pointed at each end, and used to secure the thatch on the roof. Woodworm sometimes attacked wooden scollops and to overcome this in recent times lengths of tempered steel were used instead. A wooden mallet was used to hammer the scollops home, and a sharp knife was all that was needed in their preparation – except for the twisting, which was done under the influence of steam.

There was a resident thatcher in almost every townland in the days of the thatched houses. There was one living practically next door to my grandfather, but being an independent sort of man my grandfather almost always did his own thatching, drawing from his slowly acquired knowledge of the skill. However, when the roof needed a completely new application, that merited the summoning in of the local craftsman with his considerable knowledge and adroitness.

A good thatcher relied more on practical experience than on the acquisition of a few technical tricks. All aspects of the job, right down to the handling of the straw, required a quick and steady hand and a keen eye.

To the casual observer the thatched roof of the traditional Irish home is the same throughout the country. This is not the case however, because different materials are used in different parts of the country, and different methods of applying the thatch must also be taken into consideration. In my own locality oaten straw was widely used in the old days, just as wheaten straw was used in wheat-growing areas. In the west and south, especially in the poorer regions, heather was often the only material to be had, and marram grass was used in coastal districts. Flax thatch was known in the north where the linen industry flourished, whilst rushes had to suffice in waterlogged areas.

Wheat for thatching was harvested when still slightly green so that the stalks would not be too brittle, thus yielding much more easily when handled. Some thatchers preferred to work with the straw from the winter crop, and it was essential that the straw had been flail-threshed and not put through the machine, which would damage it considerably. The best straw, in fact, was that which had been threshed by hand against a rock or threshing frame.

The coastal thatcher encountered different problems from those inland. The buildings on the coast demanded a greater degree of security and reinforcement in their roofs because the gales which swept in from the sea on a regular basis could cause havoc otherwise.

Inland, the problem was birds and their propensity for tearing at the thatch with their beaks and claws in an attempt to root out food in the form of grubs.

I can remember my father coating the thatch on my grandparents' house with a wash of bluestone to keep the birds at bay; apparently they didn't care for bluestone, though a few bold crows disregarded it with haughty disdain and proceeded as planned. A scarecrow might be made as a last defiant gesture and erected above the front door close to the chimney in a fairly strategic spot. My father relates a story of how his sister almost fell in a faint when she arrived home one evening at dusk to find 'an ould man' climbing up the roof, apparently with sinister intent. My grandfather had erected it that day and was greatly amused at her reaction!

Methods of thatching were determined not only by climatic conditions, but also by the material used and by the skill of the craftsman. A good thatcher took great pride in his work and when passing houses he had roofed little else would occupy his thoughts. A householder who didn't show active concern when his roof seemed to be rotting away would incur the local thatcher's wrath and an argument would ensue should the two ever meet. It was usual for the thatcher to return to his clients once in every five or six years to patch the roof, and every ten to fifteen years to renew the entire canopy.

In coastal areas where the thatch had to be secured with ropes and weights, the thatched roof often looked very attractive with its criss-cross pattern of ropes, or in more recent times tarred string. This lattice-work was popular in parts of Donegal, Mayo and Galway, but in other parts of Donegal and in the far north generally, the ropes were invariably fixed vertically to the roof. Originally woven from sallies, hay or straw, and for greater security bog deal, these ropes were superseded by sisal in recent times. The ropes were weighted down at the eaves by small boulders tied to the rope-ends on the gable walls only. Sometimes some of the gable-wall stones projected beyond the wall surface to accommodate the rope-ends. Wooden pegs were used too, as were iron bars in more recent times.

The thatcher, like all other craftsmen, had his own specialised tools, some of which are shown in Figure 5. For instance the yoke was used to either carry a burden of straw or to hold the straw in position beside the thatcher on the roof while he worked. The leggat was used to hammer the straw ends neatly into position at the end of a stroke so as to give a clean finish. A long-handled shears or slash-hook trimmed the thatch at the eaves, but a shearing hook was used for most other trimming jobs and sometimes even in the preparation of scollops.

Old Jack, our local thatcher, didn't carry many tools. From what my father can remember he relied almost exclusively on one knife, a small mallet, a handmade rake fashioned from a length of wood with nails hammered into it and a thatching needle. The needle was an essential tool which the thatcher used to stitch the thatch to the roof. In parts of the west where tarred string was used, it was stitched in and out through the rafters as well as the thatch, which meant that an assistant was required, working from inside by crouching in the loft. His job was to keep an eye on the ties and return the needle through the thatch. Usually for this job a special needle was required.

When my grandfather was expecting old Jack to do a job for him he generally prepared the straw himself. This had to be done some time in advance. It was carted from the stack in the haggard, unloaded and shaken out in the yard, and subjected to a considerable drenching with water. A timber plank was placed on top of the sodden mess, left overnight, then removed in the morning as soon as Jack arrived. Jack's first job was to climb the ladder to the roof and remove all the decayed thatch which was to be replaced. My grandfather would then assist him when the actual thatching got underway. Grandfather was the puller, which meant that he stayed on the ground and pulled bundles of straw from the pile in the yard. He pitched it up to Jack who placed it alongside him on the roof, preparatory to working with it in manageable amounts known as yolms. These were barely handfuls, and the first few were often referred to as 'bottles' and were placed in doubled layers along the roof at the base, their butts hanging out over the wall. Single layers were subsequently applied to ridge level. Jack, like most other thatchers, commenced thatching at the bottom right-hand corner, and worked a width of approximately three feet at a time. Known as a stroke, this was said to be a comfortable width and was more or less standard.

Jack worked in all weathers, except perhaps during high wind, blizzard conditions and heavy rains, and it was a delight to watch him during the summertime. He usually worked for about a week at any one major surgery job, and wore what he called a spangle of straw around his legs just below the knees, presumably to protect himself from the spikiness of the straw.

Jack was a good thatcher, but not a very imaginative one, preferring just the one row of decorative scollops at the ridge. This was the

---

Figure 5   A: thatcher's knife and two homemade straw-combing rakes; B: thatcher's yoke; C: leggatt, used for tidying straw ends; D: shearing clips; E: trimming knife; F: thatching spars or scollops; G: spurtles, used for patching; H: thatching needles; I: trimming knife for eaves; J: long-handled rake; K: kneecap protector for thatcher; L: decorations; M: using a yoke; N: instant yoke made from forked branch.

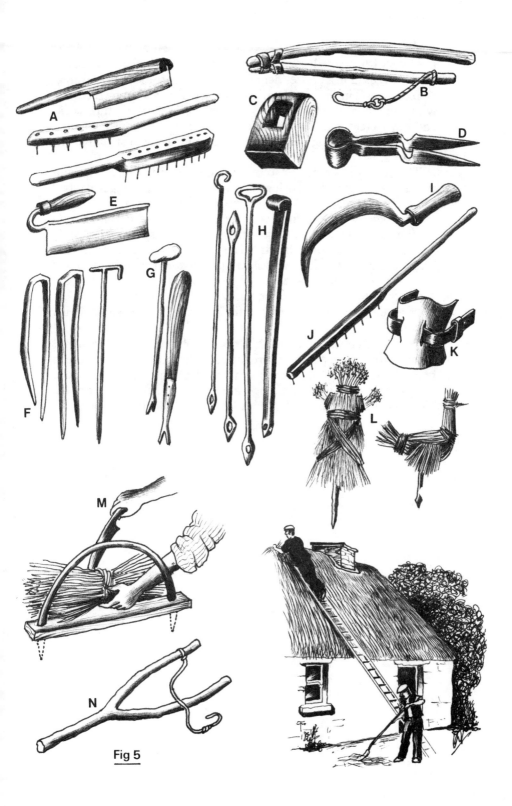

Fig 5

practice with many Irish thatchers, whereas in England ornamentation was used to a greater degree. However, in some northern areas of Ireland and in the east there seems to have been a happy medium, with some ornamentation and such embellishments as straw cocks and other creatures. Latticework was popular in the north where it sometimes ran along below the ridge and again just above the overhang.

Thatch is the lightest of roofing materials and is highly inflammable. Yet, in the old days it rarely caught fire. Steam engines posed the greatest threat when they visited with threshing mills, for they were generally parked for hours on end in the yard spitting and hissing furiously, and sending out the occasional spark which could readily lodge in the thatch. The roof would not catch fire immediately, but would smoulder quietly for days until a breeze suddenly set it ablaze and the whole building seemed to be a hot conflagration. A careful owner might have a firehook ready for just such an eventuality, averting the fire by removing the smouldering thatch.

Gutters were unknown on thatched roofs; instead the rain was thrown from a generous overhang and drained away by sloping ground. In the case of poor overhangs the rain invariably trickled down the exterior walls, creating a green stain in time, just one of the few disadvantages associated with living in a thatched house.

Chapter 2

By the Light of the Fire

The kitchen was the very heart of the traditional Irish home and its hearth-fire was the focal point, drawing visitors to it like a magnet. The warmth of the hearth, coupled with the aroma of freshly baked bread, welcomed friend and stranger alike, but when there was a parlour in the house important visitors were invariably ushered into its formal depths with due ceremony. The parlour, or 'best room' as it was called, was generally located behind the hearth wall and boasted a hearth of its own, although this was rarely brought to life with a fire of any sort, except at Christmas and Easter, or when 'the crowd from England' were staying for a holiday.

The hearth was the responsibility of the housewife and during the day she was more or less tethered to it, for not only was it a source of warmth for the whole house, but also an efficient cooker, dryer and airer. And when visitors and family gathered round it in the evening it was something to look at when the conversation waned. The fire was never allowed to go out, even at night, and was thus a strong symbol of family continuity. The housewife tended it last thing before going to bed. It was her job to pour ashes onto the *gríosach* (embers) to keep it quietly alive until morning, when a few rakings with the poker brought it to glorious life in a few minutes – decidedly an advantage on a frosty winter morning!

Turf, hand-harvested in nearby bogs, was the most important fuel source, while blocks of timber and imported coal supplemented in areas where bogs were scarce or where they produced poor quality fuel. In the west and south coal was virtually unknown as a fuel source. In the east and in the parts of the north where it was used, the hearths had to be adapted to accept coal. Strong draughts were required underneath, and these were provided by either raising the level of the hearth floor or installing a floor bellows under the hearth.

There were, of course, various types of hearth, from the very narrow to the very broad, and the very shallow to the very deep. My grandparents' wide-mouthed hearth was typical of the midlands. It boasted the usual features – the hob, the swinging crane, the deep ash-hole which had to be emptied in bucketfuls every few weeks, and the stone hearth-front where bread was toasted and the teapot was set to stand on a tripod or on a bed of *gríosach* while the beverage quietly brewed. My own clearest memory of my grandparents' hearth is of slipping from my mother's knee onto the hearth-stone and getting my hair singed! It must have been a serious disadvantage to have had an open hearth when there were many small children in the home.

The canopied hearth was also common. In this case the fire was generally set out from the wall and not in the more familiar recess. The chimney-breast wall, or canopy, rested on a strong horizontal beam known as a brace-tree, and the canopy itself was constructed from stone or wattle-and-daub. The advantage of such a hearth was that the whole family benefitted from the heat of the fire because they occupied a U of sitting space. The beam above them served as good storage space for such items as saddles and harnesses as well as a miscellany of trumpery. In wintertime onions and apples found a resting place above the hearth, and both salt and sugar were kept dry there.

In Galway the hearth often had stone seats on each side, thus forming a cosy inglenook which embraced the fire. In Kerry the hearth was often very narrow, the recess barely wide enough to accommodate the fire and its plethora of fireirons. Two wooden forms or seats were usually placed against the walls running perpendicular to the hearth, and between them they sat up to eight people. One of these forms might be replaced by a settle-bed, a seat which doubled as a bed (see Chapter Three). In those days few people were turned away from the door, even tramps. They were always invited into the home for a bite to eat and a mug of tea, and sometimes the invitation included an overnight stay on the settle-bed, which was a much-appreciated gesture on a cold wintery evening.

In parts of the north it was common to see a house with a chimney crowning each gable. Usually there were only two rooms – a kitchen and a bedroom – with a hearth built into the end wall of each. The kitchen hearth was always lit of course, but in wintertime the bedroom fire was kept burning throughout the day and night as well. A glow of warmth permeated the whole house throughout the less hospitable months.

Figure 6   A: wooden crane; B: pot-hook; C: a pair of pot-hangers; D: hake; E: old raised hearth with chain pot-hook and wooden canopy; F: open hearth with closed oven; G: metal crane; H: chain hook; I: metal crane of the type used in the midlands; J: idleback; K: early open-hearth firedogs; L: hearth with deep canopy (west and north).

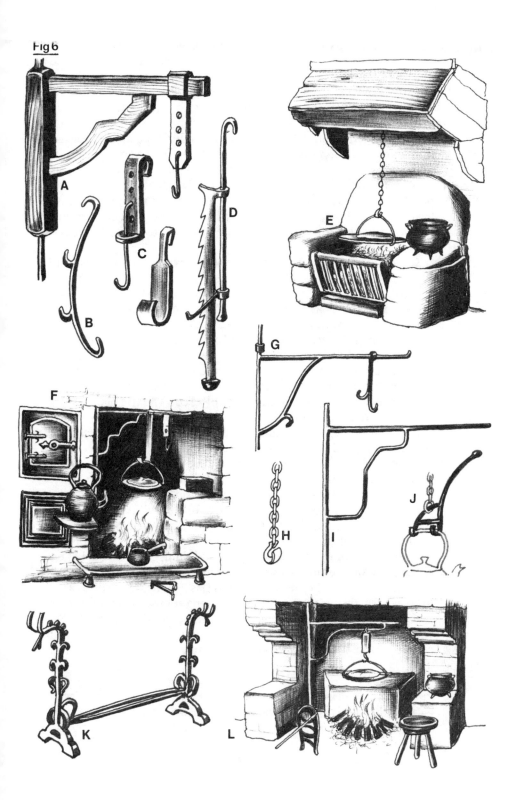

Fig 6

In the midlands and east the hearth was generally closer to the middle of the house, its chimney protruding from the thatch almost directly above the front door. The chimney wall was a huge stone or masonry affair, sometimes up to twelve feet thick, and was topped by a squat chimney stack. Because of the unbelievable width of the chimney wall the house often looked a great deal bigger when viewed from outside. Poorer quality houses might have had wattle-and-daub flues and wooden stacks, which meant that the chimney wall was never very thick. When coal was introduced as an alternative fuel the problem of chimney fires arose because coal produced a more intense heat than turf. If coal was favoured or had to be used for any reason a second chimney might have had to be built, using stone in the construction of both flue and stack.

Imported, or 'sea coal' as it was known, was the favourite alternative to turf in parts of the east and north, but in parts of Kilkenny and Carlow a local anthracite was mined for firing there. Locally referred to as 'bom', it consisted of finely ground coal and tempered clay moulded into balls and kept alight with a draught. In earlier times the hearth which burned anthracite was equipped with a narrow ground channel called a shore, which ran from the external wall on one side (sometimes both) to the hearth. In the case of two channels the one on the exposed side took over when the second one on the sheltered side was temporarily blocked. The fire blazed away furiously under the influence of such a draught, and although efficient, this method of fanning a fire to life was not as easy to control as the mechanical floor bellows which superseded it.

Other fuels which provided warmth were timber, of course, gorse, which burned very quickly and with great heat, and even dried cowpats when other fuels were hard to find. It was usually the children's chore to seek out 'cipeens' (*cipín*, 'a stick') or small rotting sticks for bringing a fire to life more quickly in the mornings. A *brosna*, or bundle of faggots – as cipeens were known in the midlands – was carried home by each youngster and dumped into a big basket by the fire for use the following morning.

One of my favourite chores as a child was helping my grandmother to collect faggots for the fire. It meant a long traipse along the hedges that criss-crossed the farm in those days, but it was good fun chucking rotting lengths of gorse or hawthorn from their resting places – usually from gaps where my father had bunged them in

---

Figure 7 A: midland open hearth; B: Donegal hearth; C: fireside, with quern on left; D: brick oven and bread-peels, used for placing loaves into warmed oven.

A

B

C

D

E

Fig7

whilst fencing. And when a particularly bad storm had blown itself out my grandmother made a beeline for any decent-sized trees in the area, hoping to amass a considerable quantity of fallen branches before any of her neighbours did!

My grandparents' hearth was set at ground level. It was therefore possible to build huge fires in it, and this my grandfather often did on a frosty night when visitors, or *'ceilidhers'* as they were known locally, were expected. A big fire was essential around Christmastime when larger than usual cakes were baked, and was also essential for boiling the 'pigs' pot'. The pigs' pot was the pot which contained an unsavoury mixture of foodstuffs for feeding to the pigs the following day. The mixture included potato skins, and sometimes whole potatoes as well, turnips, cabbage and various types of meal, and bubbled away for hours on end, almost like a witch's cauldron. The pot itself, in fact, was a large, three-legged cauldron, and to help bring it to the boil more quickly, *griosach* (embers) was heaped onto the lid. *Griosach* was also heaped onto the lids of other cooking pots, and small piles of flaring *griosach* were moved away from the main fire to form small satellite fires on which smaller pots were placed directly, as well as trivets and the ubiquitous pan which seemed to come out for almost every meal.

The kitchen range ultimately superseded the open hearth for working, and modern versions are still widely used in homes today. The transition from hearth to range was slow. In 1780 an Englishman named Thomas Robinson invented the first range which was basically an open grate with a hob on one side and a closed oven on the other. Eventually the hob was replaced by a boiler. Some of these early ranges, of which there were many different types though all basically the same, had what were known as poker ovens. The closed oven was heated only from one side – that shouldering against the open fire – and to improve conduction of heat a solid cast-iron projection was attached to the side nearest the fire. Even with this refinement the oven tended to heat unevenly and the housewife had to keep a close eye on the contents to avoid scorching on one side only. Later these hot-air ovens, as they were invariably known, were controlled by dampers.

The addition of a boiler provided hot water. The simplest boilers were filled and emptied through an opening at the top, but the more

Figure 8 A: early hearth 'range', consisting of open fire, closed oven on left, kettle-grid, ash-grate and water-tank; B: 19th c. Ulster double-flue fire; C: chimneyless hearth, of the type found in the very poor homes; D: hob-grate; E: cloam oven, a rare type of oven found in the north; F: hearth-grid; G: old fully closed range; H: range-grate.

Fig 8

sophisticated ones were equipped with a tap. A movable 'cheek' on the side of the fire prevented the water in the boiler from boiling away continuously when it wasn't needed. The cheek was simply slid in and out as required.

The next development was the closed range, which retained the closed oven and boiler, but with the improvement of a closed fire as well, a feature which was said to consume less fuel than an open fire and to retain the heat it produced for a longer period. One of the earliest closed ranges was known as the 'Kitchener' because of its alleged versatility.

Some houses retained the old-fashioned hearth even when a shiny black range was fitted in another part of the kitchen, complete with new flue and chimney stack. Others didn't bother with a range if they had a wall-oven. This was a brick-lined cavity located on the wall close to the hearth and was known since medieval times. The bread was baked on the embers of a fire lit inside the cavity some time beforehand, and, although smoky in taste, is said to have been quite good. Later on in the development of the oven the cavity was built into the fire and had a brick lining and arched roof. A long-handled wooden peel was used to insert small batches of three or four loaves or cakes at a time.

All fires carried a wide range of implements, as did the range which had to be poked to life and whose contents were invariably lifted out with tongs. In the case of the open hearth the crane was possibly the most important piece of equipment, and where absent a chimney-pole, or riddy-pole as it was sometimes known, took its place. The pole spanned the width of the chimney some distance up, out of sight, and carried all the major fire-irons, such as pot hangers and hakes, which were then suspended conveniently above the fire. The crane (*crann tógála*) of iron or bog oak, stood firmly in the fire recess and was pivoted on the left-hand side of the fire. The arm of the crane swung outwards, bringing with it substantial weights as well as inconsequential loads like a griddle or 'panny' – frying pan. The wooden crane might sound like a risky proposition, but after a very short time a considerable coating of soot left it firm and fire resistant. It carried less weight than the iron crane, and was therefore rarely found in farmhouses where cauldrons containing as much as twenty-five gallons might be used. The pot-hook, known as the hake (from the Norse word *haki*, a 'hook'), was adjustable to accommodate high and low vessels. A strong chain with S-hooks sometimes sufficed instead. Small hooks were used as pot-hangers.

Cleaning was an important chore where both hearth and range were concerned. In the case of the hearth, a homemade besom was used to keep the ashes from spreading too far beyond the hearth-stone. The ash-hole accommodated a fair accumulation of ashes, though this varied from a few days' amount to a couple of weeks', depending on the capacity of the hole, which was located behind the fire.

The bodywork of the early black ranges had to be cleaned almost daily with black lead and the houseproud housewife made a point of polishing the oven door every morning. The main disadvantage over the open fire with the capacious ash-hole was that the range required daily emptying of the full grate.

THE MIRACLE OF LIGHT

Artificial light was a rare commodity in the old days, and oftentimes the fire provided the only source of light, which was minimal when turf was the main fuel. In the west fish-oil was an important, if smelly, source of light. It was derived from the livers of shark and cod, as well as from seals, and whales on rare occasions. A mixture of salt and sunshine extracted the oil from the livers, and when skimmed off it had to be bottled and well corked.

In some areas a special vessel was used for burning oil. Known as a *slige* or crucible, it held the oil and a length of whittled rush which served as a wick. If a mobile light was required for lighting one's path in the home, a second strip of rush was drawn through the oil and set alight, then carried until it burned itself out.

The crusie-lamp, a variation of the above, was widely used in Ireland until the turn of the century, especially in the west and south. It consisted of a pair of pear-shaped dishes, one of which fitted neatly into the other. The inner vessel was filled with oil, tallow, lard, vegetable oil or even butter, and the wick which was fashioned from a strip of twisted tow or lint, was laid along the spout at the front. The lower pan collected the dripping fat from the wick; there was no waste. Primitive in design the crusie was made from cast iron in a stone mould, though smith-made crusies were also known. A long handle with a hole at the top enabled the owner to suspend it from a nail or special hook when in use.

In the west the hob-lamp and the scollop-lamp were sometimes used. The hob-lamp rested on the hob of the hearth for two reasons: first of all it provided light where it was most needed – around the fire – and secondly the fish-oil which burned in it gave off horrific fumes which could be dispelled up the chimney. The crusie lamp was also hung in the chimney in some homes, but when fish-oil wasn't used, it was customary to hang it away from the fire.

Candle-making dates back to ancient times, when cone-shaped candles were depicted in relief in Egyptian tombs and dish-shaped candles were used on the island of Crete in 3000 B.C. Throughout their history candles have been used in many different ways, including time-keeping and in religious celebrations.

Candles were produced in three different ways – dipping, pouring and moulding. The dipping method goes back to medieval times. Lengths of wick, made originally from dried rushes (called rushlights), were dipped into tallow, which had been melted down in a metal dish known as a grisset or cresset. Supported by three legs, one of which was an extension of the long handle, the grisset was sat on hot *grìosach* to allow its tallow to slowly melt. Special tongs might be used to speed up the melting process. The rushes were stripped to their pith, for it was this porous pith which was drawn through the hot tallow many times until there was layer upon layer of soft fat clinging to it to form primitive candles. A badger's skin was often used as a resting place for the drying and cooling of candles; the skin might be suspended from the rafters, hammock-fashion. Alternatively, an oak trough was used, again suspended from the ceiling with the aid of narrow straps.

A single rushlight might give thirty minutes of very poor light, depending on its length. Two burning together provided enough light for close work such as knitting or sewing. They didn't drip scalding tallow, which was an advantage over the candles which followed them. A long taper required a holder, and some of the rushlight holders were equipped with candle-holders as well. The actual rush taper was clenched between jaws called nips, one of which continued on down to a supporting block of wood or metal base.

Structurally, rushes were well designed for making light, being long and cylindrical, and absorbent. The common soft rush was used in preference to others, and it was the children's chore to collect them from fields, ponds or lakes. They were collected in late summer when mature but still a healthy shade of green. Once they turned brown, as they did with the onset of winter, they were impossible to peel.

The pouring method of candle-making involved the pouring of molten tallow onto strips of lint suspended over a drip-pan. Again it was repetitive, for it would take many layers of tallow to make a decent candle.

The moulding method was the most efficient. Known as early as the fourteenth century, it involved the use of candle moulds which could produce anything from two candles up to twenty. A two- or a

---

Figure 9 A: grisset; B: rush comb; C: soft rush; D: rushlight holder; E: rushlight and candle-holder; F: scollop light (Aran Is.); G-I: rushlight and candle-holders; J: oil-lamp; K: hob-lamp; L: crusie-lamps; M: oil-lamp; N: hundred-eyed lamp; O-P: pair of smith-made candle-lamps; Q: early candles.

A

B

C

D

E

F

G

H

I

J

K

L

M

N

O

P

Q

Fig 9

six-candle mould was general. It was fashioned from tin by the travelling tinsmith, though in more recent times tin candle-moulds were sold in small country shops. Mutton tallow was popular in the making of candles with moulds, while tow served as wicks. Also, beeswax tallow, made from a yellowish substance secreted by bees to build their honeycomb, was used. These beeswax candles were bleached and made so firm and long-lasting that they were a luxury few could afford, even though they had been used in the church since ancient times.

Tallow candles had to be tended carefully if they were to give off a generous light. Forefinger and thumb were often blackened from constant 'snotting' of the candle as the wick burnt and the flame guttered frightfully. Later, trimmers and snuffers were introduced to take care of the problem until eventually snuffless wicks were phased out when paraffin candles took over.

Candles made from the fatty acids of whale-oil were like gold dust because they didn't consume themselves too quickly, and a vegetable wax extracted from bog myrtle (*rileog*) was fashioned into candles of fairly good quality. Wax and tallow candles could be bought from chandlers who made them in batches of forty or fifty, using a battery of candle-moulds. A special candle was made as Christmas approached. This was the *coinneal mór* or big candle which shone in the kitchen window on Christmas Eve night.

With the advent of the candle came a variety of other ancillary items, such as candle-boxes, chambersticks, candlesticks, metal jugs for pouring tallow and so on. Oil-lamps were being developed, and a variety of beautiful brass lamps with decorative globes were sold for use in parlours, kitchens and bedrooms. Less decorative lamps like the tilly and the storm lamp were used in sheds and out of doors. The storm lamp, whose globe was closed, was useful on dark nights when farmers needed to check on pregnant cows or ewes. Fishermen also used it.

Horn lanterns, another type of oil-lamp, were old even in the seventeenth century. Some of them were strictly table lamps, others had handles for carrying them. There are some good examples of

---

Figure 10   A: candle-holder; B: making candles, using the pouring method; C: candlestick-holder, often called a chamber-stick; D: wooden candle box with match drawer at the bottom; E: tallman candlestick-holder; F: travelling light; G-K: candlestick-holders; L-M: wall candlestick-holders used in craftsmen's shops and in kitchens; N-O: pair of candle-moulds for domestic use; P-Q: kitchen candlesticks; R-S: candle-snuffers, used for extinguishing candles and trimming wicks.

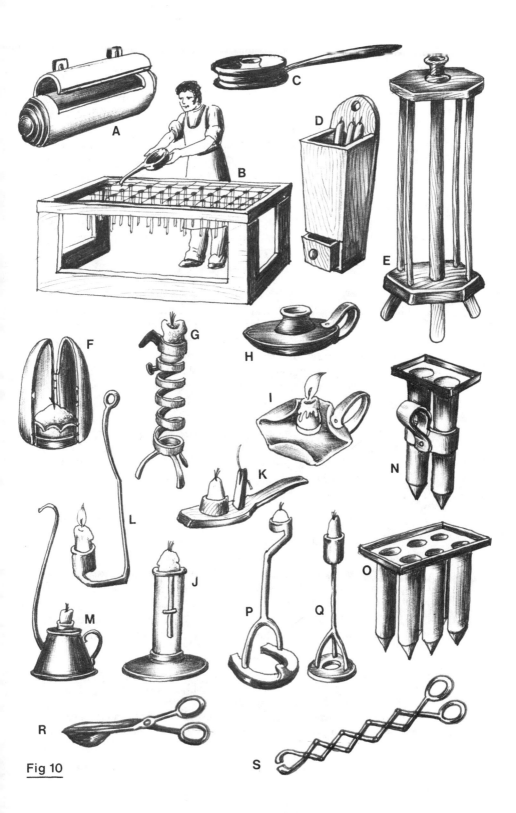

Fig 10

'hundred-eyed' and other lanterns in the Folk Museum in Knock, Co. Mayo.

When the electricity arrived, bringing with it the light bulb, it was a source of great awe to the older folk. My own grandfather displayed a comical reaction: on the night when the wiring was completed and everyone sat round marvelling at the evenly distributed light, he was last to bed. My grandmother called out to him to 'put the light out before coming up'. He grumbled and swore his annoyance, and then she heard fierce blowing sounds coming from the kitchen. When she glanced round the door to see what he was up to she found him standing on a chair blowing furiously at the dangling lightbulb. Apparently nobody had bothered to tell him about the switch!

DUDEEN AND BACCY

Finally there was another sort of light, the sort a man – or woman – smokes. Cigarette-smoking in Ireland and Britain dates from about 1860, but pipe-smoking was long established by then. My grandfather relished his daily smoke, usually reserved for eveningtime, while my grandmother and many of her contemporaries indulged in a little snuff-inhaling; some women also smoked a dudeen (*dúidín*, 'clay pipe'). Snuff was a powdered form of tobacco and because it usually induced a fit of sneezing some of the old folk believed it to have medicinal qualities; 'it cleared the head'. It was stored in a special snuff-box, or in a mull which might have been brought from a tattie-hoking trip to Scotland where the mull was first produced.

The clay pipe was the countryman's constant companion in the old days. Apart from being cheap to make, it had important insulating qualities which meant that the heat from the burning tobacco, or 'baccy' as it was known, didn't reach the lips or fingers too readily. However, they were easily broken and consequently have not survived in any great number. A good supply was vital, and, to help out, the local publican sometimes presented a free pipe with drink.

Meerschaum (from the German, meaning 'seafoam') was another cheap material used in the making of pipes, and a lot of work went into the decoration of these miniature works of art. Usually they were bought as souvenirs and hardly ever used. Faces, complete with wrinkles and hair and all the features graphically correct, made up the

Figure 11 A: tobacco-cutter; B: tobacco-measure; C-H: clay pipes; I: glazed meerschaum pipe; J: tobacco-box; K: glazed porcelain pipe; L: pipe in lined case; M: pair of tobacco-stoppers; N: meerschaum pipe made to look like old man's head; O: wide-bowled pipe; P: tobacco-cutter; Q: pair of early flints; R-S: snuff-boxes; T: silver pipe; U: snuff-mull.

Fig 11

bowls, with the smoke billowing out through a hole in the crown of the head!

Porcelain pipes were also known. Like meerschaum, porcelain lent itself very well to decoration, but was delicate, and expensive to buy. Scenes were painted by hand onto the bowl, and again it might be bought as a souvenir, or as a Sunday pipe.

A wide range of accessories came on the market for the serious pipe-smoker. A cool jar for the baccy, for example, a presser or 'finger' for compressing the baccy in the pipe-bowl, and pipe-cleaners, pipe-racks and so on. But of course the original baccy wasn't real tobacco at all, but a country substitute. When it was first intro-duced real tobacco was very expensive and beyond the reach of the peasant's pocket. So, being the resilient character he was, he came up with a plausible substitute in the form of coltsfoot, which, when combined with dried wild rose petals and other aromatic herbs, was known as *sponc*. And stiff grass stems such as those which flourish in bogs were used to clean the pipes.

Publicans sometimes provided a free pipe-cleaning service. A rack was suspended above the pub fire and the pipes were placed in it. The heat from the fire burned off the ugly tobacco stains, just as *gríosach* cleaned those at home, though less efficiently.

Some folk would argue that the dudeen caused a lot of lip cancer during its reign, so perhaps it is as well that this particular bygone was replaced by a safer pipe fashioned from briar.

Chapter 3

Furniture and Fittings

Furniture in the average home in Ireland was always basic and functional, and often homemade. Most of the decorative pieces appeared at the end of the last century.

Kitchen furniture was crudely fashioned without great attention to detail, and if the house owner was not inclined to do such work a 'handy' neighbour doubtless obliged and was invariably recompensed with a pair of chickens rather than money. A calf might be exchanged for something as big as a meal-ark or settle-bed, and a beefy bullock or the equivalent was a fair price for a well-made dresser or press-bed. An established carpenter, on the other hand, would have a set price and, unless he could accommodate animals or chickens on his plot of ground, would expect money.

The three-legged stool (*stól trí chos*) is no longer a feature of the country kitchen, but it is nevertheless familiar to most of us. It began its long history in the smoke-filled, chimneyless homes of ancient times, establishing itself there as a low 'creepie' (*stóilín*). It was essential for the family to squat low below the smoke level, so the creepie was developed for the average man or woman. A particularly tall person would have been forced to squat at ground level on a rush mat to avoid getting watery eyes, and the children either sat on the ground or on small creepies. Three legs were essential for balance because the uneven ground would easily topple a four-legged seat. In more recent times when four-legged seats took over in the home, the three-legged stool found a home in the cow-byre.

Regional styles were known, even with something as simple as the three-legged stool. Once the smoke was brought out through a chimney the legs were raised on the creepie, but not always to the same height. The seats were generally disc-like, sometimes with the tops of the legs showing through, but more often without. And one particular stool had a hole in the centre, which didn't exactly detract from its purpose as a seat but did have an advantage when one was carrying it. It was rare, even in very recent times, to find a painted stool, and varnished ones were even less common. Generally a good scrubbing was enough.

The seat of honour in the kitchen was determined not by the quality or size of the seat, but by its location. Proximity to the hearth was important, and the grandfather reigned supreme whilst he was still alive. I can remember seeing my own grandfather relaxing in his favourite seat by the hearth, listening quietly, and idly poking in the ashes with his stick. However, when visitors arrived he politely relinquished his seat and moved to a less comfortable form on the other side of the fire.

The settle-bed (*leaba shuidheacháin*) was a marvellous piece of furniture. Known as the saddle-bed or just plain settle, its exact origins in this country are open to doubt. Most historians agree that it probably came to the farmhouse directly from the medieval castle kitchens. During the day it was a box-like seat, but when an extra bed was required at night it could accommodate up to eight people, depending on size. In the larger farmhouses a matching pair was usual, one on each side of the big hearth. These matching sets invariably displayed a good deal of ornamentation, and it was not unusual to find the occasional specimen smothered in rich carvings and panelling.

Rectangular boarded stools known as forms (pronounced 'furrums' in country areas; *formí* in Irish) were popular in the midlands. Ladderback chairs were also common, and were little more than four-legged stools with backs, and again they were often homemade. The wooden seats were soon superseded by plaited *súgán* seats usually woven from twisted straw, and *súgán* armchairs were often made to match, though quite often such armchairs were kept in the parlour because of their propensity for coming undone when not properly woven.

The windsor chair is perhaps the classic 'cottage' chair, and the variety that has appeared since its introduction during the late seventeen hundreds is almost unbelievable. Essentially they were chairs whose turned legs, arm supports, backsticks and stays were all socketed into the seat, and although there were dozens of different types of windsor, they were all distinguishable as windsors.

The windsor chair is an old European type, also very popular in England where a total of five different craftsmen had a hand in the production of the one chair. Each had his own title – the benchman

Figure 12 A: form; B: boss or woven stool; C: low child's chair; D: polished windsor cottage chair; E: tall-backed commode chair; F: three-legged stool; G: low form; H: windsor armchair; I: three-legged stool with carrying hole in seat.

Fig 12

did the sawing and fretwork, the bottomer scooped out the saddle-seats with his long-handled adze, the bender put the final shape on the pieces sawn by the benchman, the framer assembled the pieces, and the finisher smoothed it off. A good craftsman could copy the windsor style, and although some of the better ones were obviously originals from England, many of the windsors which we see in old farmhouses were made by Irish craftsmen. The ladderbacks were an older type and much more common in Ireland.

The different types of windsor had different names, most of which were determined by the backrest and how it had been put in. There were combbacks, fanbacks, scrollbacks, archbacks, bowbacks, wheelbacks and arrowbacks. There were dining-chairs, armchairs and handsome rocking-chairs, and because of their strength and lasting qualities, many of them have survived to this very day and are still in everyday use. Elmwood was invariably used in the construction of the seat, the legs were turned from beech, and any remaining parts were fashioned from yew. A finish of varnish was common, though plain, well-scrubbed chairs were preferred in farmhouses where varnish wouldn't survive very long.

Enterprising farmers who didn't go in for 'those new-fangled things' sometimes fashioned dug-out seats from logs chopped down on their own land. Such seats lasted a long time, just as dug-out boats were famous for their durability. Stools and other pieces of furniture were also built in this way when money for 'proper' seating wasn't available. A plaited stool known as a boss was popular in the southeast where boss-making, or lip-work as it was more commonly known, flourished as a craft. Some of the bosses were fashioned only from straw, but a stronger, more long-lasting variety incorporated strips of bramble.

The kitchen dresser, sometimes known as the Welsh dresser because it is believed to have originated in Wales, was a feature of most farmhouse kitchens. It was the housewife's showcase, wherein she displayed her crockery, her willow-pattern delph, her well-scrubbed noggins and piggins, and a collection of ornaments and souvenirs given her by her relatives or family. And if the dresser had a very wide lip at the front it served as a place on which to lay out a corpse in the event of a death in the family. The traditional dresser had four or five shelves rising above a closed or open cupboard. There

---

Figure 13 A: swing-cradle; B: child's chair; C: low stool with four legs and rush woven seat; D: homemade ladderback kitchen chair; E: four-legged wooden stool; F: carved and turned wooden cradle; G: child's feeding-chair; H: child's chair; I: woven 'Moses' cradle; J: Ulster hinged table and ladderback chair, with low wooden stool.

Fig 13

were a great many variations because each dresser was made to individual specifications. Some dressers were as wide as ten feet, taking up virtually an entire length of wall, while others were as narrow as three feet. Drawers were fitted in later specimens, and the cupboard space was generally closed. A lot of the household trumpery was kept in this space, away from curious eyes; or, in the case of a meticulous housewife, the pots and pans.

In its earlier form the dresser was a chunky sideboard on which servants 'dressed' food just before serving. In the medieval kitchens the Welsh dresser – the sideboard and shelves combined– carried fantastic displays of copper pots, pewterware or silverware. A variation had no cupboard space beneath and no supporting boards behind the shelves.

The meal-ark was another important piece of kitchen furniture. It was made by the local arkwright or sometimes by the farmer himself, and was used as a store for flour, bran, brown meal and any other grain product used in the kitchen. Usually there were two compartments, one for white flour and the other for brown meal. The Welsh ark, known as a coffer in Wales, was introduced to Irish farmhouse kitchens where it became known as the bolting-hutch. It was designed to hold only one foodstuff, and for this reason was not favoured by housewives who used both flour and brown meal daily when baking. My own grandmother had a meal-bin – a two-compartment ark with one lid – but there were also drawer-chests which served the same purpose.

The parlour was undoubtedly for display and little else. When important visitors came to the house– such as the parish priest or local big-shot – they were ushered into the parlour with due ceremony and offered a seat in the cold, musty room, even in wintertime when they would have preferred the warmth and homeliness of the kitchen.

The parlour invariably housed a treasure of quality furniture, as well as the best oil-lamp, a well-polished wooden floor, a huge sideboard decked with clutter and organised chaos, and a myriad of family photographs (when photography became a part of Irish life in the early 1900s). Lace antimacassars adorned chintz-covered armchairs and possibly a fine windsor rocking chair, a grandfather clock probably ticked solemnly in the corner, and heavy drapes hung at the window. But for all that, a mustiness permeated the room and the grate lay empty in its classy fire surround, except at Christmas-

---

Figure 14 A: settle-bed closed for use as seat; B: settle-bed in open 'bed' position; C: press-bed; D: stepped oak dresser, also shown in section; E: typical country dresser; F: food-cupboard with pierced wooden doors; G: hen-coop with hatching and laying sections.

A

C

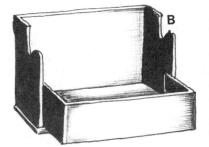

B

D

E

F

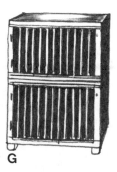

G

Fig 14

time or on other special occasions when the room would be filled with smoke for hours after the fire was lit. Of course the musty odour was sometimes overwhelmed by the spicy aroma of furniture polish and floor wax.

Essentially, the parlour was a feature of the farmhouse and not the average labourer's home, and in the majority of cases it was modelled on one of the rooms in the 'big house' or perhaps on the livingroom in the local priest's house. It was a luxury beyond the means of many a pocket, but nevertheless a part of our vernacular architecture.

Clockmaking had been established in Europe since the fourteenth century but during the 1800s new industrial techniques led to the production of cheap wall clocks which found their way into many farmhouses. However, despite their cheapness and reliability, they did not supersede the grandfather clock, many of which dated back to 1600. The grandfather reigned as king of clocks right into this century, and was often extremely ornate, displaying lavish marquetry. A plain grandfather was usually more than the average small farmer could afford, so they might have had to content themselves with a Dutch clock. This was the most basic chronometer available, consisting of no more than a white face with painted dials and a spray or two of colourful flowers, with an unprotected pendulum and chain weights.

Grandfathers were rarely taller than $7\frac{1}{2}$ ft. (2.5m). Sometimes they were even shorter, to fit in under low ceilings. The case was generally fashioned from oak, but some unscrupulous clockmakers stained their oak clock-cases with cow's blood so that the reddish sheen of 'mahogany' was achieved. These clocks had a dark face with enamel dials. Many were thirty-hour clocks, but eight-day grandfathers were known.

The farmhouse bedroom was a spartan affair, often housing little more than a bed or two, a clothes-chest and a table for the night candle. In latter times a washstand, complete with basin, jug and 'po' or chamberpot was added in deference to the hygiene demands of modern times.

Beds varied considerably in structure and design, from a basic wooden box with a sack-covered hay mattress in the poorest houses to four-posters in the big farmhouses. My grandparents and many of their contemporaries relied on brass bedsteads in the two bedrooms and the settle-bed in the kitchen, while my father can remember

Figure 15 A: large press-bed with fold-away base in use; B: truckle-bed, designed to be pushed away under conventional bed when not in use; C: press-bed with double-fold base; D: grandfather clock; E: washstand with hole for basin; F: food-ark.

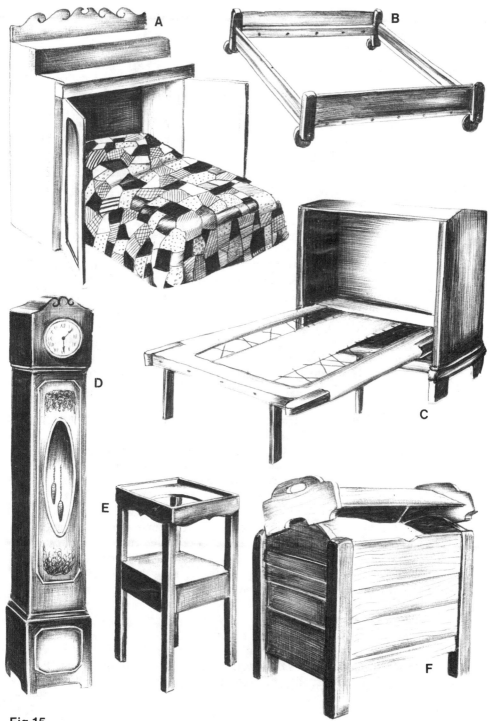

Fig 15

being banished to the loft when visitors were staying overnight. A sojourn in the loft was, I gather, an eerie experience and one my father and his brother – who usually shared the experience – didn't relish.

Some of the earliest records show that whole families slept on woven rush mats on the floor of early one-roomed houses, barely feet from the animals. In Donegal it was traditional for the whole family to sleep together in one huge wooden bed, known in some areas as the thorough bed. In damp areas liable to periodic flooding this bed became known as a truckle bed because the frame was raised to a safe height on truckles. Later, when a more conventional bed was introduced, the truckle bed fitted neatly underneath.

The press-bed was a bed which looked for all the world like a cupboard during the day, but which could be used very effectively as a bed during the night. Known in some parts of the country as box-beds they provided privacy in a crowded room if one of the family was feeling ill or peeved and needed to be alone.

The tester-bed is believed to have a longer history. It had a canopy but no sides, and was often low enough to fit in the loft, although getting it there was undoubtedly something of a challenge!

And finally there was the 'outshot' bed or bed-annexe, which was peculiar to the kitchens of the north west, although it was known elsewhere. Generally it was located on the wall adjacent to the hearth, and was sometimes referred to as the 'hag'. Two people could sleep comfortably in an outshot, but as the family grew older, and one of the grandparents perhaps grew infirm, the outshot was reserved for the ailing grandparent.

Returning once more to the kitchen, I would like to mention a few not-so-common pieces, such as a food-cupboard, for instance, used instead of the ubiquitous dresser in some eastern farmhouses. Consisting of closed or louvre-type doors, it was essentially a big press, and was probably the forerunner of other pieces of furniture, which were modelled on its basic design – the hen-coop for example, once an important feature of the south-west kitchen, and the meat-safe, whose louvred or wire mesh doors allowed just enough air in to keep the meat reasonably fresh, whilst keeping flies out.

Holders and racks were popular in farmhouse kitchens and began to be used by poorer households from the early twentieth century – egg-racks, spoon racks (which came to us from Wales where love-spoons were collected in great numbers), dish-racks and various holders for polishes, cutlery and so on. You can see a variety of these early kitchen 'tidies', as they were collectively known, in Figure 18. Prior to the 1800s such items were usually confined to the kitchens of the 'big house'.

Chapter 4

Farmhouse Fare

When my grandmother was a young housewife she never complained of boredom, mainly because she was never idle. Each and every day was filled with bustling activity. In the home she had specific chores, but because she was a farmer's wife she was obliged to help out on the land whenever she could. Usually these extra chores didn't take up much of her time, but during the busy seasons on the land – haymaking and harvesting – she often had no spare time at all. When she wasn't out raking in the field or helping to wind hayropes, she was busily occupied in the kitchen with extra cooking and baking for the kindly neighbours who arrived daily to help get the crops saved. At these times of the year other mundane household chores had to be sacrificed for a while, but at no time could either cooking or baking be put aside.

In some homes baking was a daily ritual, especially where there were large families, but in my grandparents' home baking was done twice or three times weekly. In many homes oven bread was made, that is yeast loaves, known as barm cakes, barm being the old term for yeast. My grandmother, however, didn't possess a wall-oven, so she made soda bread cakes in the pot-oven, and flat griddle bread. For variety she also made brown bread at regular intervals, currant cakes for Sundays, and boiled porter cakes for special occasions.

The preparation of food was done three times daily. In the morning my grandfather and his family were treated to a hearty breakfast of porridge, known locally as stirabout, which was always made the night before, and a mug of tea each. Sometimes a second helping of porridge would be requested again at night in times of hard work on the land when appetites were just as keen after dark as in daylight. The dinner was served in the middle of the day. It consisted of potatoes, or spuds, one or more vegetables from the garden, and meat on most days. It was washed down with mugs of buttermilk, followed by tea and well-buttered bread. The 'tay', or evening meal, was served around six, though the time varied according to the work schedule – in summertime it might be as late as eight o'clock in the evening, in wintertime as early as four. It generally consisted of a fry – potato cakes, with eggs and bacon in wintertime, something lighter in summertime.

July was a lean month in every farmhouse, including my grandparents'. Everything edible was scarce, including potatoes and vegetables. Bread was consumed in large quantities, and porridge invariably took the place of potatoes in some of the poorer homes. In Lent too, when rural folk fasted voluntarily, hunger was known, especially amongst the children. My father can remember a time when the prospect of seeing yet more potatoes without the tasty addition of butter almost made him feel sick. And the bread was dry too, and remained so in many homes. Thankfully, my grandmother made jam whose tarty flavour took the misery out of eating at teatime at least.

As far as food was concerned there was little variety at any time when my father was a boy. Rich desserts such as we eat nowadays were unknown, cakes were fairly basic – sometimes enlivened with alcohol by those who could afford such a luxury – and very little imagination went into the preparation of a main meal. Salads were unknown in most homes, whilst exotic foods from foreign parts were confined to condiments and spices, and of course the 'Ingan' (Indian) meal, a maize meal from India which had been introduced into Ireland during the Great Famine.

My father can remember having seen the maize meal in use when he was a small boy. It was yellowish in colour and came in three grades – fine, medium and coarse – usually in twenty-stone bags. The fine meal made passable porridge and the two coarser grades were blended into bread mixtures to create various alternatives to the soda bread and other traditional baked fare. For instance, Ingan ash cakes were popular in some homes. They were made by scalding a bowlful of the meal with boiling water fresh from the kettle, moulding it into a sloppy dough, and adding salt liberally. Scone-sized lumps were removed from the dough and individually enveloped in cabbage leaves, then placed in a prepared bed in the ashes. Half an hour later the scorched leaves were drawn out with the poker, and when cooled sufficiently were opened out to reveal steaming, fragrant little cakes inside. They were transferred directly to the pan for a good slow frying in butter and egg-yolk, and I'm told they tasted quite good.

Figure 16   A-C: smith-made hardening (harnen) stands for toasting bread; D: wooden toaster; E-M: single farl (quarter of full cake of bread) toasters; N: kettle-trivet; O: long toasting-stick, designed to accept four farls together; P-Q: two metal trivets.

Fig 16

In the home the woman made the bread, but in the monasteries of old the men moulded the dough and stoked the fires. Their methods were handed down, not to men but to women, who learned to use wall-ovens and make yeast loaves with dexterous hands. Many homes in the midlands possessed wall-ovens where yeast bread could be baked in batches once or twice a week. The dough was moulded in a wooden trough called a losset or *losaid*, some of which have survived and may be seen nowadays in museums, but in very few homes. It was left overnight to prove in the covered losset, expanding considerably and becoming pliable during that time. A long-handled oven-peel (see Chapter 2, Figure 7) was used to transport the individual loaves to and from the depths of the brick-lined oven.

My grandmother's method of baking was simpler because it involved neither the proving of dough nor the handling of a peel, which could be tricky when the wall-oven was very hot. She used a pot-oven, a large flat-bottomed three-legged pot with a handle for suspending it above the flames in the hearth recess. The moulded dough, which incorporated bread-soda instead of yeast as a raising agent, was placed in the pot, the lid drawn over it and then glowing coals heaped onto the lid when the pot was safely suspended from the crane. The lid ensured that no smoke filtered through to the dough as it baked.

Soda cakes were generally crossed on top with a knife; even today my mother continues to do this even though such a chore is no longer essential. It was done in former times because the baked bread, which was crusty but white when it was removed from the pot-oven, had to be toasted before the flames, and traditionally housewives toasted it in quarters. Sometimes one quarter would be toasted at a time, as and when required. My grandmother had a harnen stand for toasting a complete cake of bread at a go, but she continued to cross her cakes anyway, a throwback perhaps to other days when her mother toasted the bread in the traditional quarters.

In medieval times bread was apparently leavened with milk, a tradition which is upheld even today in some rural homes. But 'soured' potatoes – more than twelve hours boiled – were used too, as were the original true barm (a sort of yeast) made from oatmeal juice, as well as the traditional bread-soda with a pinch of salt.

Figure 17   A: three-legged cauldron and skillet pot; B: bastable pot; C: griddle and biscuit-mould; D: griddle-pan; E: long-handled skillet (British in origin); F: spit-pan; G: hob-kettle; H: copper kettle; I: sieve; J: baby-feeder; K: breadknife and matching board; L: copper jug; M: beetle; N: salt-box; O: jelly-moulds; P: butter-cooler; Q: Dutch oven and roasting-spit; R: Irish pewter measure; S: chestnut roaster; T: browning-salamandar.

Fig 17

Oaten and wheaten flour and branmeal were widely used in all areas, but in parts of Wexford an inferior barley bread was made up to the 1800s. Oaten bread was widely used as a form of payment for goods or services in times of austerity. A cake known as harran bread – formerly *aran* cake – was known in the 1600s, and is said to have been made from a mixture of barley meal and peas blended with an oatmeal dough.

Whitemeats, or dairy produce, have a long history in Ireland. Cheeses of various flavours, butter, curds and buttermilk, as well as fresh milk and cream, were consumed in vast quantities throughout history, and even today the Irish country folk are very fond of butter, milk and cheese. Hard cheese is relatively recent in Ireland, introduced when cheese-moulding became a part of cheesemaking. In fact, there are many stories of how people reacted when they saw hard cheese for the first time – most of them were certain it was tallow, for it looked and felt a little like it. Butter was made in every farmhouse, and when there was a surplus wooden tubs of it were buried in the soft, antiseptic earth of the bog. It was preserved there, slow to turn rancid, but sadly often forgotten about, for turf-cutters have frequently unearthed tubs of butter over the decades, and were pleasantly surprised at how fresh the butter smelled, although few of them tasted it.

Butter was spread liberally on almost everything, even on porridge sometimes. Fresh herbs, onion tops and garlic were blended into freshly-made butter to flavour it. Similarly, honey was used to flavour and sweeten porridge, which was served in a variety of ways by the more imaginative housewives. A milky porridge resembling gruel and flavoured with herbs was often eaten as part of the main course at midday when potatoes were scarce. Sometimes too, instead of serving porridge with milk in the normal way, the housewife served it with curds. And, when in season, wild fruits and nuts were added.

It is maintained that during the Middle Ages soldiers were sometimes paid with porridge meal, and when they didn't have time to cook it they mixed the raw meal with butter – a mixture they called *meanadhach* – and took it on campaign with them to eat whenever they felt hungry. Garlic would have to be taken along too because the raw meal encourages worms in the body; the garlic is an age-old remedy for dispelling them.

Sowans was a drink made from the husks of oats, a widely-acclaimed thirst-quencher when my father was a boy. It was made for the haymaking season when mouths were often bone dry if the weather was particularly warm. The husks were poured into a large earthenware pot, together with some whole oats and left to soak in water for up to a week. The liquid was then strained through a rush mat ready for drinking. When buttermilk was used instead of water the resulting liquid was boiled to form a jelly which was often used as an important ingredient in the traditional dish of flummery. *Práipín* was a breakfast dish made from griddle-roasted grains of wheat ground in the kitchen quern and served with cream and sugar. My father didn't know it however, though he had heard of such a dish – by the time his parents were ready to get married many of the old dishes were disappearing as the pan took over from the griddle.

It is generally accepted that the potato was introduced into Ireland in the 1590s; by the 1800s many country people had grown to depend on it to a large extent, which is why the Great Famine was such a traumatic experience in the middle of the nineteenth century. By the time my grandparents were setting up home at the turn of the century the potato was still a very important part of the countryman's daily fare. It began to form the basis of many unusual dishes, such as potato cakes, or 'tattie' cakes as they were more usually called, and boxty, the traditional dish on All Saints' Day. For this latter dish raw grated potatoes were blended with flour, milk and eggs and baked on the griddle. When eaten instead of bread for the evening meal, milk and salt might be added to the mixture which was then known as dippity. Colcannon was one of my father's favourite potato dishes, served with onion tops normally, but with kale or leeks at Hallowe'en, the traditional boxty-eating time. Butter and cream gave the mashed up colcannon a smoother texture, and in springtime when nettle-tops were blended in for health-giving purposes the dish was referred to as champ. Tattie-oaten was made from a mixture of mashed potato, fine oatmeal and melted butter, and was a favourite with children. In wintertime another firm favourite was potato soup served piping hot, straight from the skillet.

My father still uses the old terms when talking about the potato. For instance a particularly small potato is a 'poreen' and is fed to the hens, and a large floury potato whose jacket cracks open in the boiling is known as a 'laughing' spud. He also recalls how the potato dinner was always the favourite meal in his home years ago, with everyone reaching hungrily for the spuds the moment my grandmother placed them in their basket on the table. It was essential that everyone learned to peel their potatoes quickly or they might miss out, the greedy, skilful peelers hoarding up little caches of spuds on their plates before actually tucking in. Many a row started at the dinner table, I'm reliably informed.

Festive fare was a very important consideration when planning for the various festivals during the year. One of the biggest celebrations took place at Christmas, and for that no expense was spared. My father relates how Christmas was celebrated in his home when he was young. Preparations began well in advance of Christmas week itself. Food was bought in bulk, the house was given a thorough 'going-over' with dusters and brushes, and large-scale baking was done almost every day. However, nothing festive was consumed until Christmas Eve, when a specially baked fruit cake was eaten by the family shortly after the *coinneal mór* (big candle, usually red) was lit and placed in the kitchen window.

Santy came during the night, of course; in those days the toys in the sack were often homemade, and the traditional Christmas stocking was invariably filled with sticks of candy called 'Peggy's legs' and with lucky bags. Fruit, too, figured strongly, usually an orange or some other exotic fruit which might not be seen by the youngsters until the following Christmas. Early on Christmas morning the frying pan would be heard sizzling over the flames in the hearth as the traditional Christmas morning steak was cooked for the man of the house. After early Mass the housewife got to work on the preparation of the dinner. The goose or bronze turkey was cooked in the bastable (pot-oven) pot, bubbling away under a lid of constantly renewed hot coals throughout the morning. Outside in a nearby field the men and *garsúns* worked up an appetite with a game of 'shinny' (a rudimentary game of hurling) and went to their respective homes in the early afternoon feeling ravenous.

The man of the house was presented with the first huge mug of green goose soup, then the remainder of the gathering received theirs in tin panniers. The first course dispensed with, the family tucked into the main dinner, which consisted of generous slices of goose, potatoes, vegetables and sometimes a thick, greasy gravy. Porter was served to all age groups to wash the food down – a special concession to the children in some homes on this important feastday. Afterwards, porter cake was served with tea to anyone who could manage it.

The New Year was celebrated with a special barm brack, from which the man of the house took three bites in the name of the Blessed Trinity, then flung the remainder of the brack against the cleanest wall whilst uttering a prayer for hunger to be banished from the house for the coming year. The broken pieces were divided up amongst the children and wife.

On the feast of St Brigid, February 1, dairy produce was consumed in great quantities because St Brigid was the patron saint of the dairy and therefore an important saint in farming communities. Again a barm brack figured strongly, also applecakes, and colcannon was made and eaten with noggins of milk.

Shrove Tuesday, the eve of the Lenten fast, was a day of self indulgence where food was concerned – a veritable orgy of eating, as all meats and meat produce were eaten in many and varied dishes. Since the Lenten fast meant abstaining from eggs, milk and butter as well as all meats and meat-based soups, the larders were fairly well cleared out on Shrove Tuesday. The traditional way of using up the milk and eggs was to make pancakes, the tossing of which above the flames was a matter for competition amongst the young.

St Patrick's feastday (March 17) was an excuse for a break from the forty-day fast. Meat was consumed in most midland homes on that day, together with whiskey ostensibly used for 'drowning the shamrock' amongst the menfolk. In parts of the west and south fish was consumed instead, for many folk preferred not to break their Lenten fast at all.

On Good Friday dry bread and water were eaten in deference to the Crucifixion, and no animals were allowed to shed blood. On Easter morning when the fast was officially over the children went out scouting for eggs, calling at each house in the district begging for the eggs amassed during the previous forty days. They took them home, had them boiled and then took them to a selected little nook to eat them almost in secrecy. In the home the father often consumed as many as six or seven boiled eggs on Easter Sunday morning, followed by a hearty meat-based dinner in the early afternoon and rich fruit cake in the evening. Corned beef was traditional Easter Sunday fare in some parts of the country, served with cabbage and spiced with saltpetre and juniper berries. For the young people who attended the crossroads dance there was a fruit cake known as prioncam cake (from *princeam*, 'capering') and, of course, porter and whiskey flowed liberally.

There were few festivities of any consequence during the summer months, but in the autumn the Harvest Home was a huge festival of eating and merrymaking in rural communities. It followed the harvesting of the cereal crops, a sort of thanksgiving festival to which friends, neighbours and all concerned with the harvesting were invited. Meat, barrels and half-barrels of porter, cakes galore and even *poitín* flowed in abundance.

On September 29 the Michaelmas feast was celebrated with goose, and it also marked the killing of the so-called 'barrow pig' for winter use. The barrow pig was the largest in the group, and in my grandmother's time it was her job to monitor his progress up to the time of the killing, usually with a measuring tape. If he was below a certain size he might consist of more fat than good bacon. (See Chapter 12 for details on the killing of the pig).

Hallowe'en was celebrated with the traditional barm brack, into which certain items were baked in much the same way as they are today, with marriage divination in mind. Wild fruits, collected from the hedgerows (blackberries, hazel nuts, crab apples and damsons) also featured, but wild fruits collected after this time were not eaten because it was firmly believed that the *púca* (spiritual demon of the countryside) spoiled them after Hallowe'en Night. The truth was that the early frost destroyed their flavour.

COOKWARE

Every museum I've visited has introduced me to many and varied kitchen gadgets and tools used in my grandparents' time. When describing them the key word has to be utilitarian. Designs and materials were basic, but everything worked and was made to last. In Figure 16 I've shown some of the fireside paraphernalia used in baking. In Figure 17 there is a variety of cooking vessels. The three-legged cast-iron pots were widely used in my grandmother's era, but are nowadays only seen painted black and serving as flowerpots. My grandmother had three of these – a large one in which the pigs' grub was boiled every night, a smaller one used exclusively for boiling the potatoes, and a small one, called a skillet, which she used for boiling the porridge and sometimes for the cabbage or other vegetables. The skillet marked E in the drawing was a long-handled English skillet used a lot in the northern counties and around the Dublin area.

The griddle and griddle pan (Figure 17, D) were used long before the frying pan found favour in the country kitchen. Griddle bread was a very popular alternative to soda bread. It didn't rise, so it had to be made fairly thick and spread evenly across the griddle space. I'm told it was quite delicious when freshly cooked, and easy to digest – freshly baked soda bread was notorious for causing heartburn in the elderly.

Kettles were generally heavy and black. As a child I couldn't lift my grandmother's kettle even when it was empty, never mind when it was full. It was made from cast iron and was sooty black from the fire poking at its backside throughout the boiling. And it always seemed to be on, suspended from one of the pot-hooks on the crane and humming away quietly in welcome, no matter who arrived in. Copper kettles were popular too, especially as hob-kettles (Figure 17 G).

The roasting of the Sunday meat was a rare occurrence in most households because roasting equipment wasn't a feature of every

Figure 18　A: cutlery-box (Welsh origin); B: flour-barrel; C: kitchen 'tidy'; D: currant-jar; E: string-holder; F: kitchen measures; G: mortar and pestle; H: spice-rack; I: plate-rack; J: salt-box; K: wooden scoop; L: pair of noggins; M: egg-rack; N: ladle; O: meat-safe.

Fig 16

home. For instance the Dutch oven (Figure 17 Q) was known only in the better class kitchens. The meat was hung from a spit device, then partially enclosed within a metal container, opening only to the flames. A spit-pan collected the juices as they slid from the revolving meat. The poorer man's alternative to this kind of elaborate spit was the horizontal open spit across the front of the hearth.

Containers were important for keeping food and ingredients dust- and damp-free. Salt, for instance, could become soggy if it wasn't contained in a wooden box close to the fire. A salt box hanging from a nail on the wall was the norm; often it was a simple container fashioned from old pieces of wood, but sometimes a special turned container like N in Figure 17 was used and placed strategically for maximum admiration.

In Figure 18 you can see a variety of other household containers. For instance, A was a cutlery-rack, often used instead of a drawer. Originally this would have been used in Wales, where love-spoons were collected and kept on display. Here, the container was modified to accommodate knives and forks as well. Flour was kept in large meal bins, but small amounts of flour or porridge meal were kept close to hand on the dresser lip in a container such as that marked B. When there was a parlour in the house the polishing rags and polish, and the black lead used for cleaning the old-fashioned range, might have been kept in a container like that marked C. Racks were popular too – plate racks suspended from a nail on the wall or standing beside the old-fashioned sink, egg-racks for keeping eggs tidy.

The dresser was occupied mainly by delph, but there were other things housed on its shelves too on occasion. Wooden noggins and piggins for instance (Figure 18 L), which were used for holding milk and as porridge vessels. They were stave-built by the cooper and lasted a long time. Ingredient measures such as those marked F were lined up on a shelf too, and if farmers made their own herbal medicine or ground ingredients like ginger or nutmeg, usually bought whole, a pestle and mortar were essential.

Every kitchen had its share of gadgetry, a good selection of which is shown in Figure 19. My grandmother didn't have much time for such 'new fangled' ideas, restricting her gadgetry to a meat-mincer and probably a sugar-cutter, though my father cannot remember having seen one in the house. Sugar-cutters were essential when

---

Figure 19 A: sausage-maker; B: meat-mincer; C: early whisk and bowl; D: garlic-press; E: lemon-press; F: kitchen all-purpose knife; G: nutmeg-grater; H: spice-grater with box; I: coffee-mill; J: knife-cleaner; K: sugar-cutter; L: pair of inhalers; M: knife-grinder; N: meat-press; O: herbal-tea maker; P: nut-cracker; Q: knife; R: nut-cracker.

Fig 19

sugar was bought in tall cones of solid crystal and had to be broken down with a hammer, then sliced. Coffee came in bean form, so a gadget was necessary there too; a coffee-grinding machine with a blade for grinding up the beans into a coarse powder. All kinds of squeezers were known – lemon and garlic presses, orange-juice squashers, and meat presses which were used to make beef tea, a popular beverage with the older folk. Jelly was made from earliest times from bone-stock and boiled calves' feet, most often for savoury dishes, but when honey was added it made a welcome sweet. Jelly made from aspic which best suited moulds was introduced in the 1800s, and jelly moulds fashioned from tin, copper and delph were used to create dramatic and unusual, if wobbly, shapes.

Small gadgets included cherry-stoners, marmalade-cutters, apple-corers, ice-shredders and bone-mills. And, of course, there was a variety of meat-mincers.

The knife-cleaner was perhaps the most unusual piece of kitchen equipment. Until recently I had seen only the large table cleaner (Figure 19 M), whose internal wiry brushes cleaned the inserted knife blade (see position of arrow) when the handle was turned. But then in a local museum in Athlone I discovered a small, much more manageable knife-cleaner (Figure 19 J). The reason for having a knife cleaner at all was because knives tended to turn black after continued use, and a cleaner which incorporated a grinding mechanism was an added bonus for the knives tended to get blunt quickly too.

Keeping food fresh was a problem in hot, sultry weather. In the 'big house' an ice-house might have been established somewhere in the grounds, but farmers who couldn't afford the luxury of a piece of ice, never mind an ice-house, generally buried food temporarily in the coolness of the earth. Meat-safes, fashioned from wood with a wire mesh panel in the door, kept meat and other perishables out of reach of flies in summertime, and butter-coolers and delph tureens kept butter and cheese reasonably fresh in the dairy.

Food was generally bought in bulk, especially flour, tea and sugar. My grandmother lived in an area where she could purchase a 'pennort' (penny's worth) of this and a measure of that – the size of the measure being predetermined by the shopkeeper. Tea might have been bought by the chest coming up to Christmas, and flour always came in flourbags, which were utilised afterwards to make flourbag sheets and vast aprons, while a good tea chest might become a clothes-chest or end up holding tools in the barn.

The 'van' is still a feature of some rural areas, including my own. But in the old days it wasn't an engine-powered van, but rather an elderly hawker with a horse and cart. He touted for business in areas where farmers and others didn't get much opportunity to go shopping in a nearby town. His cart was always loaded with an unbelievable selection of stuff. For the housewife there were, of course, plenty of food items she might need, including pre-packed lumps of sugar, brown paper bags filled with tea, bread-soda and other ingredients, as well as fly-ridden flitches of bacon, strings of sausages, enormous black puddings and other meaty items. Sewing needles, threads and other hardware would be included too, as well as panniers, tin cans and kitchen tools. My father and his young brother always made a beeline for the sticky penny-buns, eager to spend their hard-earned pennies on feeding themselves with the unusual confections.

On the once-a-month fairday the children spent much of their time in the town staring longingly at exotic foreign fruits, candies and confections in the shop windows. If they were lucky they might get a length of tooth-shattering sugar-stick, or a Peggy's leg, or even some hard toffee. Both fruit and chocolate would have been beyond the reach of their pockets in those days.

Tea-shops were great meeting places in local towns when my mother was a young girl, and, of course, the pub has always been popular with the menfolk.

Chapter 5

Homecrafts

Craftwork was an integral part of the rural community in early times because clothes and other cloth items were all homemade. Up to the 1930s a travelling tailor made suits for men, and what the housewife could not make herself, she had the local 'manty maker' (from *maintín* meaning 'mantua maker', a mantua being a cloak) sew up for a small fee. However, sewing was virtually obligatory for young girls who usually learned the craft at their mother's knee.

SPINNING AND WEAVING

Weaving is as old as civilization itself, although the early looms were doubtless badly made and produced poor quality cloth. Only the very wealthy would have had machines capable of producing tapestries, fine rugs and soft fabrics. By the 1800s ordinary farmers could afford the luxury of a good quality loom, so that finer fabrics were being produced for the lower classes. The fibres used were usually indigenous, such as flax (linen), wool, and some wild cotton, although imported cotton was woven extensively around Prosperous, Co. Kildare, and imported silk was blended with wool to produce a fabric called poplin woven in the Liberties area of Dublin and parts of Cork.

Weaving was usually man's work. The raw material had to be spun into manageable fibres and this was done by the womenfolk, who spun and carded. The spinner was often an elderly woman living alone and depending solely on the pittance her spinning brought in. If she was an efficient worker and was doing well, she could afford to buy her own wool from the farmer, but if she wasn't she would 'steal' it from the hedgerows and fences where the sheep had lost hunks of their fleece in scratching or passing from field to field.

Sheep are resilient animals that thrive on poor land, and because of this the western half of the country has always been sheep-breeding country, and consequently spinning and weaving country. In the early twentieth century the spinning and weaving industry was probably at its peak because by then almost every home in sheep rearing country possessed a spinning-wheel or a loom of good quality. The annual shearing, when the sheep were stripped of their warm fleeces, was an important event in the life of a farmer from the western mainland or from any of the islands along the western seaboard. The wool was collected, bundled into bales and sold to spinners, weavers or wool merchants, depending on the locality and the amount of wool. And of course some of it was kept for the farmer's own use.

The shearing took place from mid-June onwards (see Chapter 12), and different sheep produced different quality wools. For instance Galway, Roscommon and Scottish Blackface sheep were all mountain sheep and produced long wool suitable for carpets and certain homespuns. Galway 'Muttons' and Wicklow Cheviots produced a medium wool suited to ordinary homespuns like shawls, petticoats and tweed for men's suits. But the Suffolk Down, a popular English introduction, was strictly a lowland breed with dense, short thick wool, ideal for sorting and with very little waste. Fine tweeds were made with this type.

Once the shearing was completed the farmer graded the wool. A single fleece produced three distinct grades – the 'diamond' quality wool from the animal's back, the lesser diamond from around the legs and above the tail, and the 'stragleens' from the very edges, which was invariably discarded.

The spinner washed the wool. The fleeces were carted to a nearby stream or well and washed as one might wash clothes, until all pieces of briar, mud, dung, dead leaves and grass were thoroughly removed. The fleeces were swished in the water to avoid tangling and felting, two serious problems which developed when wool was badly treated.

When the wool was dried it had to be oiled. This could be done with goose-grease or, in more recent times, with paraffin-oil, and was necessary if the fabric was to be waterproof. If coloured fabric was desired, the dyeing process took place before the oiling. The ancient Irish peoples loved bright colours and these they derived from natural sources such as roots, leaves, berries and flowers, all of which produced a harmony of colours which no chemical dye of modern times can rival. Among the plants used were lichens in Donegal and Mayo, collected by children from rocks and boulders to produce various even dyes called crottle and scratloch, and heather, which produced a clear yellow dye. Yellow flag iris produced a dull black, while dull red was derived from the wild madder plant. A deep blue came from a plant named woad or *gláisín*, and a plant named rud produced a crimson dye. Rich black was achieved by soaking the wool for a time in a boghole, or by boiling it in bog water. Chips of oak added to the water gave an even glossier black, and a mixture of indigo and urine produced a blue-black. The flowers of the ragwort (the *buachallán buí*) or those of the gorse (*aiteann*), were used to produce brown. Oddly enough, despite the 'forty shades of green' in the Irish landscape, green dyes were hard to produce, and, until the advent of chemical dyes, all the greens were dull lacklustre shades. Consequently, green was considered unlucky, especially where clothes were concerned.

When the plain or dyed wool was ready the spinner settled down at her wheel to spin it into a continuous fibre. Prior to the invention of the spinning-wheel, the spinner spun by hand with a spindle (see Figure 23). A spindle – sometimes fashioned from wood from a tree of the same name – consisted of no more than a length of stick with a weight at the end, usually a piece of glass or a stone. Called a whorl, it served as a flywheel.

The *túirne mór* was the big spinning-wheel, or wool spinner. It consisted of a large wheel on a simple platform with the spindle works positioned at one end, directly opposite the wheel. In some areas, the platform was low, so the spinner could sit while working, in others it was raised and the spinner stood beside it. The smaller treadle-wheel was used a lot in Donegal and the north generally, where it was originally introduced to spin flax. Twisting and winding on remained two separate operations until the introduction of the U-flier, and the treadle meant even more improvement because the spinner's hands were free to work the wool at all times. By respinning she could produce two-ply wool for heavy garments, and if she was spinning for the local weaver she invested in a niddy-noddy or click-reel to skein the wool; otherwise she rolled it into balls, and sometimes kept them on a reel-pole beside her. When using either the niddy-noddy or click-reel she measured the wool into skeins, weighing set amounts. She had to keep a mental record of the wool fed onto the niddy-noddy, but a click-reel kept turning until a certain number clicked and she knew she had enough.

Next came the carding, which was done with a pair of carding boards or with the seed-heads of wild teasel tied to a makeshift frame. The carding boards had rows of little curved teeth which opened and straightened the fibres by brushing them between the boards. The fibres were then fluffed up and made to lie in one direction only, and were finally rolled by hand or by the smooth parts of the boards into a

---

Figure 20 A: Aran woman, with drugget skirt doubling as shawl in emergency; B: spool-rack; C: heron scissors; D: thread-pack; E: darning hand cooler; F: hemming-bird; G: wooden clamp; H: chatelaine; I: pair of needle-cases; J: example of plain patchwork; K: table lockstitch sewing-machine; L: lockstitch sewing-machine with treadle and stand.

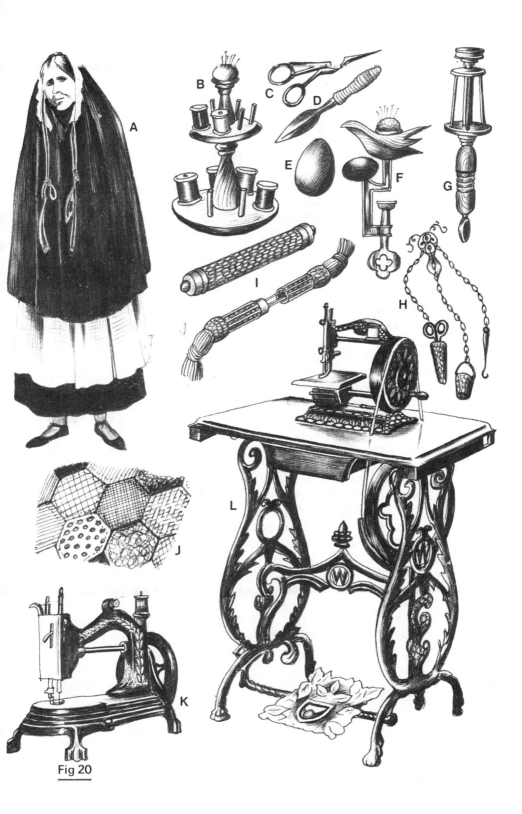

Fig 20

tube-like shape called a rolag. It was now ready for the spinning-wheel.

Flax was next to wool in importance, and although a few sporadic crops were grown in the extreme south, it was mainly confined to northern counties. The crop was harvested when the blue flowers were passed their best, gaited or stacked in the fields, retted (allowed to rot) in a lint-hole, and finally gaited again until the flax farmer was ready to cart it to the linen mill (see Chapter Nine).

The scutching mallet was used to make the fibres more pliable, though a special flax-breaker was much more effective. The fibres had to be combed, and for this a hatchel was used. When it was removed from the hatchel any remaining bits of fibre were known as tow, and were either made into candlewicks or burden-ropes. The flax was stored in bundles known as stricks until the spinner needed them.

In boggy areas the poorest spinners collected bog cotton for spinning. They also used it for stuffing pillows when goose-down was not readily available.

The loom was the implement of the weaver, varying in size from the small handloom to the huge floor loom. Few homes boasted both spinning-wheel and loom, for the weavers generally worked as a small village community and the spinners worked from outlying cottages. In Donegal, Mayo, Galway and the Aran Islands weaving was an important industry in the 1700s and 1800s, and is practised today in many areas. A weaving community was generally made up of the spinners, a dyester (traditionally male) who dyed the wool expertly, a group of 'clothiers' or weavers, who lived close to each other or to a tuck mill, a small milling business powered by water.

Traditional Irish clothing, which survived up to the 1920s in some rural areas, was made from wool or linen, with ceremonial garments and some Sunday best fashioned from silks or satins. Donegal produced practical tweeds, dyed dark, and often bearing stripes, checks and plaid patterns. Similar quality was produced in Mayo, but the colours were traditionally brighter. Galway produced the famous *báinín*, or white flannel, and of course Kerry homespuns were poorly acclaimed for they lacked imaginative design and decent colours, although Kenmare tweed was held to be very good.

Figure 21 A: flax spinning-machine; B: flax distaff; C: distaff with flax fibres (linen) wound on ready for spinning; D: flax beating-machine; E: pampootie shoe (Aran Islands); F: Aran folk dressed in traditional Aran clothes — *báinín* cap, sweater, *crios,* trousers with leg split for pulling up easily in water, pampooties, Aran shawl and black skirt; G: carding-horse.

Fig 21

Needlework incorporated the use of needles and included many different and specialised crafts. Sewing was perhaps the most basic needlecraft, and in my grandmother's day virtually every girl could make her own clothes, although the services of the local dressmaker were called upon if a woman needed a costume or coat made. Few women had the benefit of a sewing machine at their disposal, or the benefit of electric light. A workbox or basket housed the needle-woman's paraphernalia – cotton reels, scissors, pins and needles, and so on. And some women had a chatelaine which hung from a button by a small hook and contained a thimble, scissors in a small case and stitch-picker. A hemming-bird or wooden clamp held material to the table when it was being sewn, and a wooden darner was used when darning socks or woollen garments.

Patchwork was an important craft in the old days. The needle-woman used a combination of patches of old discarded garments, backed with flourbags for extra support, to produce quilts, cushions, or shawls. My own grandmother did this type of work, but her favourite patchwork involved crocheted 'Afghan' squares sewn together to make a quilt (see Figure 22).

American 'log-cabin' patchwork was known in Ireland as folded work, and calico or flannelette was used as backing. Mosaic patch-work consisted of geometrical shapes and looked like a neat jigsaw when finished. When octagons or other awkward shapes were desired they were first traced on to cardboard and cut out so that the shapes would be roughly the same size throughout the pattern.

Appliqué patchwork set no rules. Total freedom of design meant that this type of work suited all standards of needlework, both the artistic and the clumsy. Motifs such as birds or flowers cut from chintz were common, and the edges were always left 'raw' with herring-bone stitch finish.

Quilting – not to be confused with patchwork quilt-making – was another old craft. The quilt was made by securing three layers of material together by through-sewing stitching in decorative patterns. A pricking tool marked the patterns beforehand.

Whitework flourished throughout the 1800s. Muslin was a favourite material for summer garments at that time and lent itself very well to embroidery of this kind, incorporating white sprigs or even more elaborate patterns, always in white.

Figure 22 A: cottage floor loom and flying shuttle; B: click reel; C: woman of 1700s wearing hooded cloak and drugget skirt; D: drugget skirt; E: old woman spinning; F: big wool-spinning wheel; G: reel-holder; H: crochet needle and Afghan square.

Fig 22

Men's suits were invariably made by the travelling tailor. Some clothing could be purchased at the stalls on fairday, but these didn't always fit correctly, so, when possible, suits were made by the tailor. He arrived in the district from time to time, bringing with him his goose-iron, his special ironing-board if he had one and his box of needles and other tools, and it was traditional for the client to provide board and lodgings as part of the fee for the suit.

LACEWORK

Whitework, already described above, was a form of needlepoint lacework, but genuine lace was made on a cushion with bobbins and was called pillow-lace in Britain and bone-lace in Ireland, probably because the earliest bobbins were made from bone. The pillow was well stuffed with feathers or hay; tightly-packed straw was the favourite material. The centre of the pillow sagged with use and often had to be 'middled' (refilled at the middle). When not in use it was covered with a protective dust cover called a heller or hindcloth.

The pattern for the lacework was pricked onto parchment with an old needle fitted into a wooden bobbin, and the pins which followed the pattern were always rust-resistant brass, and were known by various names, such as limmicks, bugles and kingpins. The bobbins varied considerably, but all were decorative, often enhanced with coloured beads, shells, etc. Domino bobbins were decorated with little spots. A young man often had 'I love you' or some such message inscribed on a bobbin for his ladylove.

A bobbin-winder was used to feed thread onto the bobbins, but this was a luxury most lacemakers didn't have. Instead they wound the thread by hand, a long and tedious job.

Embroidered net, such as whitework, was known as Limerick lace, and in the area around Carrickmacross lacework known as cutwork was made by sewing through a sandwich of paper pattern, muslin ground and machine net. When the sewing was completed the pattern was torn away and the muslin cut to leave a delicate sprinkling of flowers or whatever on the net. In the area around Mountmellick yet another type of whitework was known. A strong white cotton thread was worked on a linen base to sketch delicate floral patterns.

Figure 23 A: lacemaker's horse; B: lacemaker's pillow; C: selection of lace-making bobbins; D: sample of Irish lace; E: Aran crios belt in the making; F: wool comb; G: flax hatchel; H: reel-winder; I: carding-boards; J: hand-spinning; K: a wooden niddy-noddy, used for winding wool; L: knitting-sheath; M: small hand-loom.

Fig 23

In some parts of the country, particularly damp localities, rushes were used in craftwork. Principally they were used for making St Brigid's crosses to celebrate the feast of the patron saint of the dairy on February 1, and although similar rules and traditions were known throughout the country, different crosses were known in different regions. The rushes had to be pulled and not cut – that was essential if the charms it was to carry were to work – and it was important that they be pulled on the eve of the feastday. The girls made the crosses, then sprinkled them with holy water and placed them above the door, on the dresser and in the cow byre. Traditionally, three-legged crosses were hung in sheds in the north west, and when rushes were not available, straw or some other material sufficed.

Straw was used in the fashioning of corn-dollies for the harvest celebrations in autumn, when boys were encouraged to present them to girls. Nowadays they are still made in Britain for sale in craft shops and I managed to pick up a traditional lantern dollie, which was known here too. Oaten straw was simple to use but too soft to last long, and barley straw was too short to work with; both wheaten straw and rye straw were long and excellent for plaiting.

TRADITIONAL IRISH COSTUME

Traditional Irish costume, or peasant costume, was determined by the hardship endured. Shabby clothing was the norm on land, even for the womenfolk, and the children were often forced to dress in cut-down adult clothing or cousins' cast-offs. I can remember seeing my grandfather clad in hard-wearing striped shirts, heavy-duty but shabby trousers, tied at the legs, and hob-nailed boots. And my granny wore a black shawl, heavy-duty flared skirts, big starched apron, a couple of wool jerseys and black boots or laced shoes. Paisley frocks were popular in the summer when the weather was hot.

The hooded, Kinsale-type cloak – black with red satin lining in the hood – was popular during the last century. *Báinín* cloaks were common in the west, while on the Aran Islands a beautiful shawl was worn. Red or blue striped petticoats were worn with the 'linsey-woolsy' or drugget skirt, both of which came to within five inches above the ankle and no higher until the early 1900s. Black druggets were often doubled as shawls.

The white lacy cap worn by married women was known as the *caipín lása* ('lace cap'), and a *binneog,* or kerchief, was worn when out working in the fields. In summertime sun hats woven from rushes and muslin bonnets were popular, especially with young girls.

Among the curiosities were the 'Paddy Martins' or footless stockings, which my grandmother knew as *troighín* (from *troigh,* meaning 'foot'). They were designed for wearing in wet weather when continuous flapping of a wet skirt against the legs could cause blistering. In boggy areas pattens or leather brogues mounted on platforms were worn when traipsing over peaty land. Leather shin-guards called leggings were used when working in the fields. They were drawn over flapping trousers to prevent them from getting in the way of dangerous machinery.

The Aran Islands had their own distinctive costume. The men wore sailor-type trousers with a slit on the outer side of each leg, thus enabling them to pull them up over the knees when wading in the sea. Flannelette shirts and chunky, oily Aran sweaters were worn to keep the strong winds and rains at bay. Each family was known to have its own combination of Aran stitches so that a fisherman washed ashore following an accident at sea could be identified. The *crios* was the traditional woven belt for holding the trousers secure and the pampooties were the leather slippers worn on the feet.

Mainland people once wore rawhide slippers similar to the pampootie. They were made by the brogue-maker from a single piece of rawhide called a kip, and sold in large quantities at the local fair. Clogs with wooden soles were also worn in some areas, and some clog-making tools can be seen in Knock Folk Museum and in Muckross House Museum.

In more recent times, flourbags were made into shifts for young girls; cotton was fashioned into smocks like those worn by men in rural England up to the 1800s and wool was knitted into all kinds of garments. In those days of self-sufficiency nothing ever went to waste – even an old discarded jacket was taken to the field and mounted on a pole to scare the crows away from freshly sown seed, and old woollen garments made excellent floor cloths!

Chapter 6

Dairy and Laundry

Over the years two important chores have evolved in the country home – dairywork and the weekly wash. In ancient times too, butter- and cheese-making were important chores, but they were relatively straightforward tasks compared to the dairywork known even in my grandmother's time. And the weekly wash is a fairly recent intro- duction, as you will discover later in this chapter.

Both these 'new' chores required more of the housewife's time, more of her energies, and sometimes more space than the house allowed. A new dairy might have been built, or a new wash-house, depending on the number of machines and vessels involved. It is amazing how many different kinds of churn and washing-machine were brought onto the market at the turn of the century and how many vessels and miscellaneous tools were known for these two specific chores.

THE DAIRY

Not every farmer could afford to build a dairy, so in the vast majority of cases the dairywork was done in the coolest corner of the kitchen. However, before the actual dairywork could commence the milking had to be done, and until recent times this was always the woman's work. During the summer the milking was done out in the field, but in wintertime and for much of the spring the animals were housed in the byre and were milked there. Sheep, goats and donkeys were also milked, especially by the poor. During the milking, goats and sheep

---

Figure 24 A: early milking-machine; B: milk-separator; C: dash churn with plunger attached to lid; D: early ice-cream-maker; E: milk-separator; F: swing churn; G: wooden butter-ladle; H: butter-stamp; I: goat-milking churn with seat attachment; J: ice-cream scoop; K: butter-pats; L: butter- marker; M: pair of butter-stamps; N: churning with the dash; O: washing the churn after use; P: pot-bellied dash churn.

Fig 24

were stood on special wooden milking-stands and given food to keep them occupied for the duration.

Milking vessels varied, from simple wooden pails to special metal milking-cans with various refinements, such as a seat low enough for milking a goat in the field. The tinsmith-made 'tinny' was also used, though it was originally meant to be a water-carrier. Pails were carried more easily with the aid of a shoulder-yoke, made from ash, willow or sycamore and carved in such a way as to fit comfortably on the shoulders and balance the burden of the weight above the carrier's arms (see Chapter 7, Figure 33).

Once in the dairy the milk was poured from the pails into a large earthenware vessel to cool. When there was a surfeit of milk some of it might be sold fresh in the local village; the farmer's son often travelled from house to house with a donkey to which a metal five-gallon can was strapped, together with a pint measure used for measuring out exact amounts.

One of the biggest worries in many areas was how to prevent the local 'hag' from stealing the butter. This heinous crime was not committed in the usual way, but through the work of special charms, invariably carried out in secret on May morning. In some areas it was firmly believed that the hag worked in disguise, usually that of a hare, sucking the teats of victim cows so that they would produce only creamless milk during the remainder of the year. If an old woman was seen gathering the dew on May morning she was suspect. Therefore, it was only right that a farmer walked his land on May morning to watch for trespassers on sinister missions. The dew was gathered with a cowhair spancel – a tether used for tying a cow's front legs together during milking – which the hag had previously stolen from the farmer's cowbyre. By uttering the words 'Come all to me!' as she collected the dew she placed a charm on the spancel. Afterwards, while she secretly gloated, the farmer's wife spent hours churning in vain. The hag's churn however overflowed with butter!

Other *piseogs* centred around the business of butter-making too. St Brigid's crosses were hung close to where the churning took place as well as in the cow byre in an attempt to ward off the charms of the hag. Holy water from various holy wells was sprinkled on the animals at Eastertime, and twigs of rowan tree or elder were suspended from the rafters in an attempt to keep all kinds of evil away. And the power of blessed salt was sacrosanct.

Many folk believed that the milk from a red cow was superior to that of the milk from any other, no matter what the breed, and the red poll (a hornless red cow) in particular was highly prized. The thick yellow beestings (post-birth yellowish-coloured milk) was often valued above the milk itself, and was a favourite when making eggy pancakes. Suspicious people offered it to the fairies instead, leaving it in a shallow dish by a lone bush to 'appease the wee folk'.

The poor fairies had a lot to answer for in the old days. When a cow was mysteriously ill she was said to be elf shot, and when the local quack vet arrived to examine the beast he produced the 'missile' by sleight of hand from the vicinity of the cow's belly – the missile being an arrow-head, once used by our primitive ancestors. Also known as flintstones, these early weapons looked lethal enough to have been flung by angry elves, but of course they weren't. Nor were the fairies responsible for damaging a building because it had been built on a 'fairy's pass', even if 'poltergeist' activities did occur and animals housed in that shed died for no apparent reason. Oddly enough though, the real reason hasn't been established either!

BUTTER-MAKING

Generally, butter-making was a weekly chore, unless the farmer had a lot of cows, a well-equipped dairy, and sold butter in large quantities. The milk had to be three days old before churning could commence. The cream was skimmed from the top and ladled into a second vessel, then covered with muslin while it 'ripened'. The milk left behind in the earthenware crock was now known as skimmed milk.

By the early 1900s the milk-separator was a feature of most dairies, for it saved a lot of time by eliminating the overnight ripening process. A centrifugal force within the machine separated the light-weight cream from the heavier skimmed milk so that they poured out through separate channels.

Once the cream was ready, the churning took place, and this was accomplished with one of many different types of churn. By far the most popular churn was the dash or plunger – so called because the operator plunged the agitator (dash) downwards into the cream. It was stave-built and varied from 2 to 3½ feet (just over 1m) in height, and the shape varied enormously, from narrow cylinders and splayed vessels to pot-bellied varieties. Generally they were bound with iron or withy bonds and had their lids fitted in place with two iron clasps. The agitator, also known as the beater, the staff and the stick as well as plunger and dash, had its handle protruding through a hole in the centre of the lid. The beating end varied from region to region – sometimes a round disc with holes, sometimes a cross or H of wood.

Glaik churning was a complicated method of churning known from Cavan northwards. A spring arrangement worked the dash, and a sort of see-saw worked a lever when the person using it moved her weight.

Other early churns included the swing churn suspended from the ceiling and pushed about to agitate the contents, and the rocker churn, which agitated the cream when rocked furiously. The former was used almost exclusively in the area around Lough Neagh, while the latter was an introduction from England, also known in the north.

My grandmother had an end-over-end churn, also known as a barrel churn because essentially the cream-holder part of it was a stave-built barrel. A handle turned the barrel, and three iron clasps held the lid firmly in position. Progress could be monitored by peeping through a spy-hole located in the centre of the lid. Triangular end-over-end churns and boxlike types were also known, and not all of them had four legs either – I've seen one in Knock Folk Museum with a squat wooden stand. Table churns generally had a smaller capacity and were therefore owned by small farmers who didn't require a lot of butter from a single churning. And, of course, breakfast churns barely produced enough butter for a single meal, as their name suggests.

Very large churns, worked by horse-power, were often seen in the big farmhouses. These were probably the first to disappear when the creameries were set up around the country, because the big farmers with the substantial herds were the first to bring their milk to the creamery.

Butter-making was a serious business which didn't end when the churn was washed and put away. Before being removed from the churn the butter had to be perfectly 'grained' — thick and ready for moulding — then it was removed and washed several times in clear cold water. Butter-workers like those shown in Figure 25 took the drudgery out of the washing in the early 1900s. A grooved surface sloping away to a drainage hole took the surplus buttermilk (*bláthach*) from the butter as the roller was turned. Less efficient was the butter-press, which squeezed the water from the butter when pressure was applied.

Once the butter was 'clean', butter-pats were used to mould it into pound shapes, butter-balls or wedges, onto which an emblem was imprinted with a special butter-stamp. Some emblems were symbolic and special to the family, but the majority were thistle-heads or swans or even grazing cows that merely enhanced the appearance of the butter when it was being sold. Stamps varied from press-on types to rollers, both of which are shown in Figure 24.

Figure 25 A: table box-churn; B: neckless dash churn and plunger; C: barrel churn; D: dash churn with small glaiks attachment for easy manipulation; E: ceramic dash churn and plunger; F: butter-scoop; G: end-over-end churn; H: butter-worker; I: narrow 'cottage' dash churn; J: cream-bowl; K: butter-scoop; L: butter-worker; M: butter-scales; N: butter-press.

Fig 25

Luck played an important part in butter-making, for the business was fraught with unseen dangers. Predictably, the fairies were blamed when anything went wrong – such as butter that wouldn't 'break', which was actually caused by milk not separating properly due to 'heavy' weather. A neighbour who called during the butter-making was always expected to say 'God bless the work' on arrival, and then work the dash or crank handle (depending on type of churn) before leaving so as not to 'take the luck'. Beggars were sent from the door during the churning and told to return later, and if a neighbour requested the loan of a tool or vessel for whatever reason during the butter-making he was considered bad-mannered!

CHEESE-MAKING

The making of hard cheese wasn't known in Ireland until the end of the last century despite our history of eating curds, soft cheeses and butter. For a long time country folk thought hard cheese was tallow when they saw it in the shops, but by the twenties and early thirties cheese-making was a familiar occupation in many homes, particularly in the south and east.

It was made thus: untainted milk was poured into a large wooden or metal vat and left overnight to ripen. Then it was slowly stirred and rennet was added as the temperature rose to 80°F (rennet is a foul-smelling reddish-brown liquid, either bought in small earthenware jars or prepared by boiling the lining of a calf's stomach). Stimulated by the acid in the milk the rennet coagulated it and this process was helped further if stirred constantly with an agitator. The milk was now known as junket (giuncán) and following a rest of thirty minutes or so it was thick enough to slice with a knife. The junket was cut up into a cracked mess with a pair of special curd-knives, then scalded. When left to settle for a second time the thick curds rested at the bottom and the whey rose to float on the top. It was drained off and the remaining curds was left to ripen. A curd-mill was then employed to grind it into tiny granules, to which salt was added, thus completing the actual preparation of the cheese.

Pressing was a long-drawn-out affair which followed in most cases where good-quality hard cheese was required; otherwise the cheese was simply moulded into blocks and eaten immediately.

The cheese was compressed into moulds and placed in a lever-press, a pressing instrument which appeared for the first time during the late 1800s. It was superseded by the spring press in the twenties and thirties. Pressing meant a lot of extra work, and was usually common only in the Golden Vale and other cheese-making areas where hard cheese was produced commercially. The cheese was made solid in the press, then stored away in a cool room where it had to be turned once a day for the first two weeks – twice daily in clammy weather – and every five days or so afterwards.

Ice-cream was made during the 1800s, albeit in very small quantities. A bucket-shaped ice-cream-maker was introduced for use in the 'big houses' during the mid 1800s where they had an ice-house and small portions were sometimes given as a treat to the workers at harvest festivals and so on.

WASHDAY

A relatively modern development, the weekly wash was an important part of my grandmother's weekly timetable, but was hardly of any significance to the generation which went before. Nor was personal hygiene. After all, why bother washing the body when the clothes weren't clean?

During the fifteenth and sixteenth centuries washing was a twice or three times yearly event, but by the late 1800s the weekly wash was establishing itself as an important household chore. The 'big house' had a laundry complete with laundering gadgets and vessels, and now the more well-to-do farmers were following suit by building wash-houses and equipping them well.

Water was often a major problem, however, especially when the home was miles from a decent water source. Farmers sometimes could afford to sink wells in the yard, but the majority of country folk had to either take their dirty laundry to the nearest river or lake, or fetch water from the river to the house to do the washing there. Either way it was cumbersome and time-consuming.

In the event of using a tub, the housewife trampled barefoot on the laundry until all the dirt was removed. When she had no tub she used a bat, known as a bittle or *slis*, to pound the draped garments against rocks or a convenient grassy bank. A strong implement made from oak, the *slis* was superseded in most homes by the 'dolly' during the late 1800s.

The homespun fabrics used in the garments of the day took the bittling well, but were inclined to shrink in the process. In damp weather they shrank even more because they were exposed to dampness for long periods. Drying was a serious problem, especially in wintertime, not only because of the inclemency of the weather, but also because the garments were heavy and took a long time to dry at the best of times. In summertime the garments were simply strewn over gorse bushes which held them firm in the breeze, but in wintertime, they were either hung out in the barn on a rope, or taken indoors to the kitchen and draped on chair backs around the hearth.

Homemade soap was made from a plant called soapwort, which produced a lathery liquid when boiled. And of course there was

83

carbolic soap in the shops. Before the introduction of washing soda, lye was made from white wood ash, which helped to soften hard spring water. Rain water, however, was used where possible.

The washtub was basic to every household. Made from wood or metal, it varied in size and make and often doubled as a bath for the youngsters on Saturday nights. Dollies and possers were introduced for use with tubs – the dollies serving as beaters, the possers as 'suckers' of dirt, though the word 'poss' was an old English word for 'thrust' or 'trample'. The washboard was either rubbed vigorously against the dirty garments (see Figure 26), or was held firmly against the body while the garments were rubbed vigorously against it, depending on the type used. A special copper pot was sometimes reserved for boiling clothes and soiled linen.

The very first washing-machine was invented in 1782 by a man named Sidgier. It consisted of no more than a rotating drum operated by a geared handle, and was the principle used in many of the old wooden washing-machines which were around during the second half of the eighteenth century. Many of the later ones had wooden mangles attached for wringing the washed clothes out after rinsing. In the 1860s an Englishman, Thomas Bradford, set up a machine-making business, and his rotary washer (see Figure 27) was one of the best of its kind at the turn of the century.

Mangles came in all sizes and styles – from the 'ribbon' mangle, originally designed for wringing priests' collars, to the big cumbersome stone mangles, which occupied whole corners of laundries. Mangle-bats were also known. Originally used in Scandinavian countries, they were useful for mangling small garments prior to ironing. The garment was wound round the roller, which was then drawn over the elaborately-carved battledore to extract both water and creases. Lacy caps and *binneogs* (working caps worn by women) were mangled and crimped in a machine which combined mangle and crimping irons (see Figure 28). Alternatively, they were mangled with the mangle bat and crimped on a crimping-board or in a crimping stack.

Stretching was often necessary to prevent shrinkage and this was often done by using tenterhooks. The hooks were attached to a bar between two uprights, weighted at the bottom by a heavy object.

Figure 26   A: pair of bittles; B: American type washboard; C: washtub with washboard incorporated into bodywork; D: using the washing dolly; E: pair of washing dollies; F: using the washboard; G: early wooden washing-machine; H: rocking washing-machine — *c.* 1900; I: wooden washer with ringing-wringer attached — operated from the front; J: blanket-washing posser; K: drum washer — *c.* 1920s.

Fig 26

It wasn't until the sixteenth century that Europeans began to use a heated implement for taking the creases from clothes and bed-linen after washing; thereafter many tasks previously performed with a mangle were now done with an iron. The Chinese had already been using open-pans for centuries. These open-pans were filled with hot coals and drawn over the fabric until every crease was obliterated, and a few of them have been used here in Ireland in the past. Early irons were often massive tools, especially the goose-iron traditionally used by the tailor. The box-iron and the sad-iron were the two most commonly used irons in Ireland at the turn of the century, and although the box-iron seems like the more sophisticated of the two, it was the first to be invented. Shapes varied, but the principle was the same: an iron slug was shaped to fit the hollow body, which had either a hinged or sliding heel or top for access. A housewife needed only one iron and two slugs, which were heated alternately during the ironing.

The charcoal iron was heated by burning charcoal within its body, with the fumes escaping out the side through holes. Later a funnel took the fumes further from the laundered fabrics. To keep the charcoal embers alight within the iron, the instrument was swung backwards and forwards. The sad-iron, or flat-iron as it was sometimes known, was made of solid cast iron, and was heated before the flames of the fire on a trivet. In some of the larger farmhouses, iron-stoves were used to heat a large number of irons together.

The first paraffin irons appeared in the late 1890s, then came Naphtha irons, which burned methylated spirits, and petrol irons – veritable bombs I would have thought! Coal gas was used during the 1920s, and, although efficient, it was dangerous because the housewife inhaled dangerous fumes. In the 1880s the first electric iron was introduced in America, but electric irons didn't find a foothold in Ireland until the 1930s and 1940s.

Specialised irons were introduced for special work. Starched linen was sometimes ironed with a very hot glossing iron, and glazing could be achieved by rubbing the material with a highly polished 'slick' stone or a shaped piece of glass, or with a Welsh invention – the glazing calendar. Sleeve and flounce irons reached into deep sleeves

Figure 27 A: pair of iron-stands; B: Thomas Bradford's revolutionary washer of the 1800s; C: pair of irons in coal heating box; D: tailor's goose-iron; E: goose-iron stand; F: box-iron on metal stand; G: wooden iron-stand; H: sad-iron; I: cuff and collar iron; J: charcoal iron; K: slug iron; L: early electric iron; M-N: petrol irons; O: charcoal iron; P: electric iron; Q: travelling iron (box, stand and slugs); R: horseshoe iron-stand; S: slug iron; T: charcoal iron.

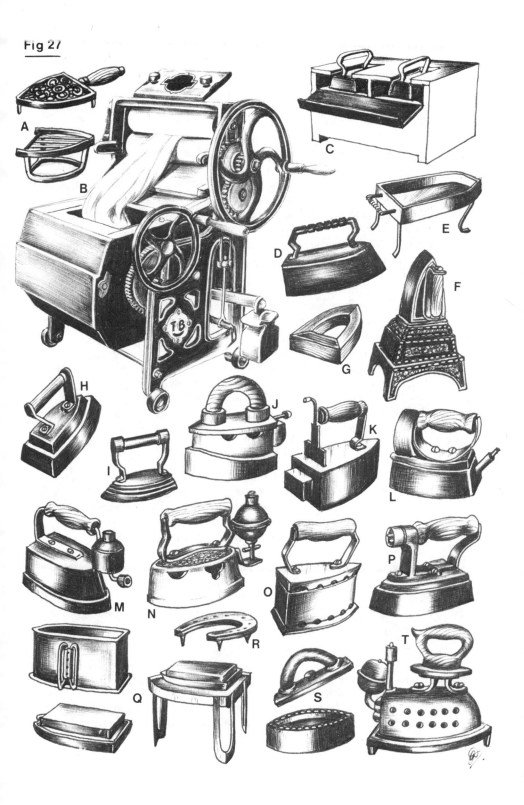

Fig 27

and pleats, and of course there were hatter's irons which weren't of any special use in the home.

Standing irons were widely used in Ireland in the 1800s. They were mounted on stands and were used in the upright position for skilled finishing. An egg-iron consisted of a solid egg-shaped piece of iron mounted on either a wooden or metal stand and used for finishing the tops of sleeves and waistbands. The so-called Italian iron, known in Ireland as the 'tallon iron', consisted of one or more cylinders of brass or iron heated by alternating pokers, which had been wedged into the open fire. Those made in the 1700s were particularly elaborate and were often stood on polished mahogany blocks. They were used for crimping fine lace edges and frills, and were particularly suited to ironing velvet. The cap-crown iron had a circular or half-circular top of iron or brass and it too was used for specialised work. Travelling irons, used mainly by well-to-do ladies, had to be light, and were therefore fueled by petrol or methylated spirits. There is a good example shown in Figure 27.

Three-legged iron-stands were widely used to accommodate the still-warm iron when not in use. Homemade stands were often fashioned from cast-off horseshoes, but bought stands could be extremely elaborate. An iron-hanger was hooked over fire bars in range-fires, and could hold two flat-irons, heels down. Long-handled charcoal ladles held the charcoal in the fire as it heated, and an old piece of wool blanket was invariably used to grip the handle of a hot flat-iron when in use.

PERSONAL HYGIENE

Feet-washing at night has long been a tradition in rural Ireland, but other hygiene wasn't popular until the end of the last century. Wooden tubs were used on rare occasions as baths. It was traditional in some areas to bathe the whole body once a year in the May-morning dew. And young girls were known to wash their faces in dew each morning in order to have a flawless complexion. Buttermilk, too, improved the complexion, as did egg-white, while the water in which potatoes were boiled was used to remove stubborn dirt from skin. Men who suffered from chilblains took their boots and socks off in the bog and allowed the antiseptic turfy soil to clear away the cause of the itch. Tonics made from herbs got to the root of certain skin

Figure 28 A: soap-stand; B: poss stick; C: early clothes peg; D: making lye; E: bar of homemade soap; F: ribbon and collar wringer; G: stocking stretcher; H: wooden dolly; I: hem iron; J: washboard; K: large laundry wringer; L: early box iron; M: Chinese iron; N: crimping iron; O: tallon iron; P: crimping iron; Q: egg-iron; R: tallon iron; S: pair of tallon iron slugs.

Fig 28

problems – herbs such as hawthorn, stinging nettle and chickweed, all of which improved the quality of the blood.

The hair was washed regularly, especially by young women who often wore it to the waist. Egg-yolk was a natural conditioner, and a plant named cleavers was boiled to make a marvellous hair-tonic. Hair colourants were also known: the juice of marigold flowers turned the hair blond when used constantly, tea gave a rich coppery brown, daily washing in goat's milk or tobacco kept greyness away, and the juice of elderberries gave dark hair a rich glossy shine.

The 'doctrine of signatures' held firm where herbal remedies were concerned – if a plant resembled a part of the body then it must cure it! So, when wrinkles appeared in the face, the juice of primroses and cowslips was used to remove them – just look at the leaves of those plants!

The 'Croppy Boy' of the old song was a product of the 1790s when young men wore 'cropped' short hairstyles. Long hair often attracted lice, which necessitated its cutting, or the use of paraffin-oil or garlic-oil, which wouldn't endear one to the masses! Men have worn beards, on and off, since the beginning of time, depending on trends. In the 1850s beards returned to popularity after centuries of clean-shaven faced and waxed moustaches. Saturday night was the traditional time for shaving at the weekend; it was considered bad luck to shave on a Sunday. And it was bad manners to shave or have a hair-cut on Good Friday. In parts of the west, men believed that they must have all their hair on the Day of Judgement, consequently they kept all their hair-cuttings in a box, together with nail cuttings and teeth.

The so-called 'cut-throat' razor was invented by a Frenchman in 1762, and if not used properly, it could do just that! Then in 1895 an American, King Camp Gillette, invented the safety razor. He thought the constant sharpening which was necessary with the cut-throat could be eliminated, and he was right. His safety razor and disposable blades were a godsend to the busy man with little time for rasping a blade on a sharpening belt every morning.

Soon the shaver had a variety of accessories to choose from, such as shaving brushes to apply lather to the face before attacking it with the razor, and shaving mugs with compartments for one or two brushes and some soap.

Figure 29   A: pair of cut-throat razors; B: honing stick; C: strop (honing strap); D: honing stick; E: dandruff-combs; F-I: early razors; J: shaving the old way; K: washing baby; L: hip-bath; M: crimping-stamp; N: Scandinavian iron; O: sink board mangle; P: moustache wearer's cup; Q-R: pair of shaving mugs; S-T: shaving brushes.

Fig 29

Chapter 7

The Land

When landlordism was abolished in Ireland we became a nation of small farmers, with each tiny parcel of land standing as an independent unit within the community. Nowadays many of these original farms have been merged to make bigger farms, and consequently many field boundaries have been obliterated from the landscape. When I was a child my grandparents had a total acreage of something under twenty acres, and that was considered a decent farm then. Today, my own father's eighty or so acres seems meagre; if my grandfather had had that much land he would have been the local squire!

THE GEOGRAPHY OF THE LAND

The farmhouse, the yard and the outhouses formed the nucleus of the farm, with the land stretching away on all sides. Sometimes the farm was broken up and spread out within a townland or even within a few townlands, and usually the bog was located well away from the main farm. *Bothairíns* (boreens) linked various fields and plots of ground, and the Mass path linked an entire townland with the local church.

The farmyard was a feature of lowland farms. It was a centre of activity, where the horse was yoked, the hens fed, the farm foodstuffs prepared and the corn threshed. It was central to everything, located as it was like a courtyard amongst the sheds and farmhouse. My grandparents' farmyard was typical of others in the midlands. It ran the length of the thatched house, had sheds opening onto it from two other sides, and a wall running the length of the third with the twin stone piers and iron gate smack in the centre of it. A dungheap (*carn*), which was carted out as manure to the land once a year in springtime, was located within sight of the settle-bed where my grandfather normally sat; the dungheap represented what little wealth he had, so he liked to be able to see it when he was relaxing. The yard cockerel greeted the morning from the summit of the heap, his loud raucous cheer echoing for miles, and the hens found it a convenient source of food.

Sheds and outhouses varied from region to region. In the midlands and east, where farmers were marginally more well-off than their western or southern counterparts, the number of sheds was greater on each farm. My grandfather, for example, had a pig-house, a shed for the ass, a barn which doubled as a cart-shed, a cow-byre for four animals, and a couple of sheds for calves of varying ages. The hens too had to be housed, as well as the turkeys and geese. Originally, makeshift shelters sufficed, but during my childhood proper sheds were provided. However, the more sheds a farmer had, the more cleaning out he had to do, and although my grandfather was a placid, unconcerned sort of individual to talk to, he was as fastidious as the next man about keeping his farmyard and sheds clean and airy.

The sheds were generally built from wattle-and-daub, or wattle on its own, except in the coastal areas where stone was used for building everything. And where the farm was devoid of decent cover for animals, small huts were built in the bog or elsewhere. In mountainous areas fox-resistant stone was used to build hen-houses, and in parts of the east and midlands brick was used in the construction of pig-sties which incorporated pig 'runs'. Cow-byres were always low and dark. Wooden or clay partitions separated the cows during milking and a cobbled channel took the urine away to a shore outside the building. Hefty chains attached to the wall above the mangers were tied around the cows' necks to prevent them from wandering. In wintertime the cows were confined to the cow-shed throughout the day in particularly inclement weather.

Hen-houses varied from small makeshift huts accessible to the fox to big, well-built, airy buildings with plenty of nesting space and roosting poles. Hens, however, are inclined to be independent and often lay their eggs anywhere except where they should. A deserted manger, a sheltered spot in the garden hedge or amongst bulky sacks in the barn were all good places to look when eggs weren't appearing in the nests provided (see Chapter 12 for details on homemade nests).

Turkeys, when bred by the farmer, were housed separately from the hens, and the geese and ducks were usually housed together in a small shed opening off the farmyard. My own strongest recollection of my grandmother's geese was of the big noisy gander taking after me if I stepped onto his territory. He was the menace of visitors, hissing and honking in a threatening fashion, and because he saw the lough (the small lake in front of the house) as part of his territory he acted like a watchdog when anyone so much as ventured round the corner of the road. Consequently, my grandmother always knew when a visitor was coming.

The (corn) barn-cum-cartshed, either had wide doors which opened out or no doors at all. A loft, which provided extra storage space, was a wonderland of delight for imaginative children, who played there in bad weather. The farmyard gateway was usually dignified by a pair of massive piers, either square or pyramidal with rounded or conical caps. The farmer was proud of the entrance, and, come springtime, the houseproud farmer spent some time whitewashing the piers and painting the gate.

Field-gates were often unique, with no two in a townland looking exactly the same. Wooden ones were usually homemade and would resemble no other gate anyway, but even the smith-made gates followed no standard pattern, although there was an accepted method of installation. They had to swing forward like a fire-crane, directly on the heel, on a projecting iron spud which swivelled in a stone socket. The handle was simply drawn into a slit in the pier and couldn't be locked as such; a tightly drawn chain could be used to secure it in the closed position. But field-gates were often no more than a 'stick-in-the-gap' (*stopallán*), consisting of a heavy pole which was drawn across an open gap at a height considered resistant to animals. When barbed wire became freely available to farmers they invariably used it to make improvised field-gates, as well as strong resistible fences (see Figure 31).

The haggard was the storing place for hayricks and cornstacks, and was generally located on high ground behind the house and farmyard, and was reached by a cart-track from the yard. In flat country, platforms would have to be built for the ricks and stacks, otherwise flooding could undermine them. Another feature of the farmstead in the old days, and located close to the haggard – often beside it – was the kitchen garden, where produce for the table was grown. Traditional cottage herbs were important for flavouring plain food, fruit bushes produced the raw ingredients for jams and chutneys, and fruit trees provided edible delights for the children.

Crops were separated from the animals in the fields by field-barriers, usually referred to as ditches. A hedged ditch (*fál*) consisted of a barrier of earth faced on one side with large stones. Hawthorn and bramble were encouraged to grow through the cracks between the stones to form vigorous thickets and render the barrier stock-

---

Figure 30 A: squeezy-stile; B: wooden stile; C: haggard-stile; D: ladder-stile; E: well-shelter (Co. Clare) and praying stick used by pilgrims; F: open well; G: gate-pier; H: zig-zag wooden stile; I: stone wall-stile with wooden crossbar and uprights; J: round stone pier; K: wooden field-gate; L: smith-made iron gate hung between square stone piers.

Fig 30

proof. The double ditch was a feature of my own part of the country. It boasted a width of at least ten feet (3m) and was often as tall as eight feet (over 2m). The path running its length was used by pedestrians in times of flood, and was a favourite route to the fair with animals because the double ditch recognised no townland barriers.

In the west and south stone was the obvious material when it came to constructing barriers. Stone walls of varying density and design criss-crossed the western counties in a network of effective barriers, and on the Aran Islands stone gates were known as well, although the word 'gates' is probably erroneous in this context because there wasn't, strictly speaking, any gate at all – part of the wall could be dismantled and rebuilt again as required. The other stones in the walls were also arranged loosely so that cows or sheep wouldn't dare touch them for fear of bringing the whole wall toppling down on top of themselves.

The stone barrier associated almost exclusively with county Galway was the dry stone wall similar to the Scots galloway dyke. The lower half was constructed from overhanging boulders. In county Clare, Liscannor stone was used in precision-built walls as well as in the more haphazard constructions, and the large flat slabs of grey, slate-like stones were used for roofing as well. Stone barriers also had their own features such as the sheep's pass, which was a small hole in the wall, just high and wide enough to let sheep pass from field to field whilst keeping the other, bigger animals confined to one field. A keeping-hole was a nook in a wall with a slab or wooden base, and it was used for storing large pots, and so on. A similar nook was used for housing one or more bee-skeps (see Chapter 12).

The wayside stile was a feature of the east and midlands and parts of the country where barriers lacked gates in any quantity. A well-trampled path led to and from the stile. The stile itself, whilst on one person's land, was essentially a right-of-way, and there might have been as many as twenty stiles in one townland – each one, of course, occupied by a banshee or spirit of some kind once the witching-hour arrived at night! The stile was also a traditional meeting point for courting couples during the early part of the night.

There were different kinds of stile. The latch-gate stile was familiar

---

Figure 31 A: barbed wire field-gate; B: pole gate; C: field-shelter; D: hen-house, constructed from stone with thatched roof; E: stone wall adapted to accommodate gate; F: zig-zag field-stile; G: wrought iron field-gate hung between pair of stone piers; H: wooden field-gate, often adapted to serve as harrow when no longer suitable as a gate; I: country pump surrounded on three sides by stone wall, with foothole behind pump to facilitate owner of field beyond.

Fig 31

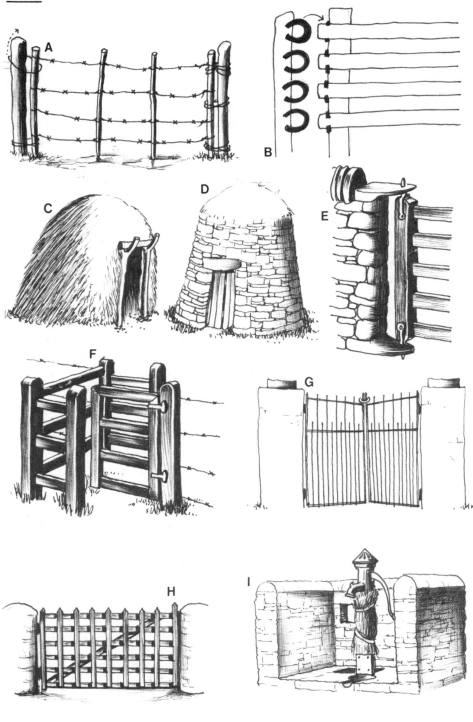

at the entrance to churches and churchyards, but wooden and stone stiles were more familiar on farmland. And with the advent of barbed wire, wire stiles were used in haggards and on wire fences. Ladder-stiles were often used where fences were particularly high, such as with the double-ditch barrier of the midlands.

Townlands were usually defined by rivers or streams, especially in lowland areas. Spanning the rivers at certain points were 'kishes', or footbridges (*droichead coise*). Most of the kishes were only a single plank in width, but when the river separated one part of a farm from another, the kish would have had to be wide enough to take a cart. A series of planks tied raftlike together formed this kind of kish, and two hand-rails of rope bordered it on each side.

The bog road was a feature of peaty country, where it often swept across the landscape like a primitive highway, for it was frequently high above ground level to avoid flooding. It was a lonely road, and usually a fairly long and straight one, and although used on and off at all times of the year by pedestrians, it didn't come alive until the autumn when the farmers carted their harvest of turf from the bog to the farmyard.

The well, especially the holy well, was a very important feature of the rural landscape. The ordinary well was often the only source of drinkable water for miles, and if it was believed that it had once been visited by a saint and was therefore declared a holy well, all the better, because holy wells were known to carry valuable 'cures'. A few of the more important holy wells were used as shrines, and woe betide the man or woman who used the water for domestic purposes! Any water taken from a shrine was 'blessed' and could be used only as a cure or for sprinkling round the house to keep away evil. On Pattern Day crowds of country people congregated at the nearest shrine to pray, using notched prayer sticks.

In more recent times ordinary wells were often topped by a draw-well with a rope and crook for the bucket, or by a mechanical pump. The village pump became the traditional meeting place for the women of the locality, just as the smithy was the traditional meeting place for their menfolk. In country areas the pumps were sited at the side of the road in their own little concrete platforms with a concrete or stone wall surrounding them on three sides. A hole in one of the walls gave access to the field beyond.

Figure 32   A: wooden gate-pier; B: large stone shed, once a dwelling-house, adapted to accommodate carts as well as animals, etc.; C: Tacumshane windmill, Co. Wexford; D: bog shelter; E: lean-to added to dwelling-house to store turf; F: watermill, Co. Roscommon.

A

B

C

D

E

F

Fig 32

In the west the soot-house was a common feature, and on Achill Island the remains of an old soot-house can be seen. Separate from the farm, yet part of it, the soot-house was home to the family for almost six months, when they lit fires day and night to make soot. The soot gathered as smoke lodged in the chimneyless roof, and when spring came round the whole roof was removed and carted to the fields to serve as fertiliser. A new roof was put on for the following winter when the whole soot-making process began again. When visiting the West Highland Folk Museum in Kingussie in Scotland, I was interested to discover that this tradition was also known on the island of Lewis, where the houses were called black-houses.

Ireland is criss-crossed with interesting little narrow roads, even in mountainous and boggy areas where one doesn't really expect to find them. The vast majority of these were originally horse- and cart-tracks or pedestrian pathways which became rights-of-way between townlands and farms. The transport which travelled on these at the turn of the century was rather primitive and undemanding, so it wasn't until the forties and fifties that a lot of them were properly maintained for modern transport.

Getting around wasn't exactly a problem in the old days if one didn't hope to get too far; certainly, travel beyond the parish one lived in was rare, and beyond the county boundary was out of the question unless one had a good pony and trap. The only people to really travel were those hoping to find work, and their search often brought them to America or England. Travelling for pleasure is a relatively modern concept, although shopping trips to Dublin were known in my grandmother's time. Such a trip would have been the subject of discussion for weeks – not only in the home but also in the local village and in other people's homes, where much speculating was done. Most travelling was done locally, and unless the whole family was travelling or some merchandise was being transported, it was done on foot. I know of a man who thought nothing of walking the fifty miles from central Westmeath to Dublin because he didn't have the fare for the train.

For travelling on the farm, from farmyard to field and so on, the farmer had the donkey and drey or the horse and cart, or the slide-car in earlier times. The slide-car was a sort of large slipe or sledge with shafts. It was pulled along with a draw-rope or chains and could transport fair quantities of sticks, sacks, stones, or whatever.

Figure 33 A: *fáinne* for head to help balance a load; B: back-pannier; C: carrying load on the back; D: carrying wooden pails with help of shoulder-yoke; E: back-basket; F: creel-basket; G: creel-basket; H: gurry-butt for use in the yard; I: gipsy vardo.

Fig 33

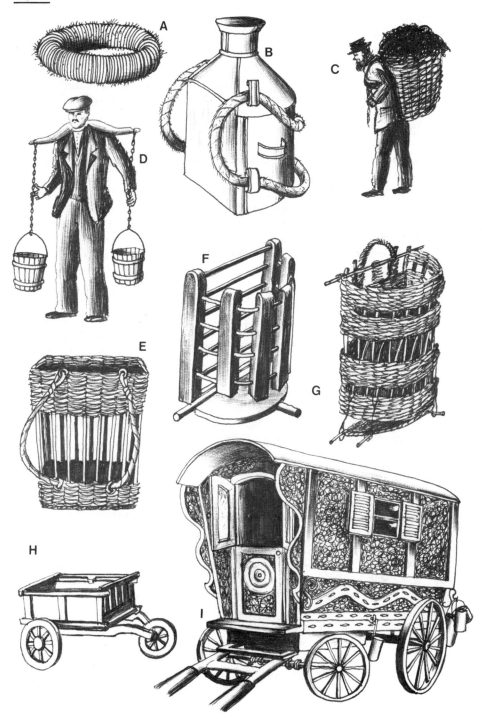

However, the lack of wheels meant there was a great strain on the animal pulling it. A cross between the cart and the slide-car was known in my own area. It consisted of a platform about four feet in length and two in width, and had rollers underneath to prevent it from sinking in marshy or boggy terrain.

Block wheels were used as long ago as 400 B.C. in Ireland – the term blockwheel describing any wooden wheel made from two or more pieces of timber fastened together with dowels to form a disc. These apparently very primitive wheels were used in Ireland until recently, but with an axle. The wheel, as we know it, was added to slide-cars to make wheel-cars, and then the box-cart or Scotch-cart was introduced and virtually took over in a few years. As its name suggests, the Scotch-cart is a Scottish creation, and at the beginning of the nineteenth century it is said that Scottish wheelwrights and cartwrights were brought over to Ireland to show Irish cart-makers how to make it. One of its chief advantages was that the sideboards could be removed; they could also be replaced by tall, slatted boards on fairday. When wickerwork sideboards were used they were known as *ciseáin*.

In the west the usual driver of a donkey and cart was an elderly woman buried under a black shawl, with a dudeen planted in her mouth. A ready tongue and a belt of a thorny stick were enough to control the donkey whenever he became recalcitrant. And if that method of restraint didn't work, she leaped from the vehicle and flung her wool drugget skirt over the unfortunate animal's head!

E. L. Walter, in *The Fascination of Ireland* (London 1913), mentions the 'pookawn' (*púcán*) which was to be found in Donegal. Fashioned like a Galway hooker it bore a Spanish-type sail and could be seen 'sailing' about the moorlands of Donegal until the last century.

A classier mode of transport was the trap, which was used by midland and eastern farmers for family outings. Originally, the trap was designed for the governess who liked to take her charges out for the occasional trip in the countryside, and it was known as a governess cart. Then when farmers started using it, it became known as a 'swanky trap' because it seemed infinitely more stylish than the average farmcart. There was seating for at least six – three facing three – and access was through a door at the rear, which dipped down and had a metal step. I can remember being driven to Mass in a

---

Figure 34   A: basket slide-car; B: wooden pre-Famine cart; C: wooden fair-going cart with upright laths; D: slide-car; E: cart-jack; F: early Scotch cart; G: wooden field-cart; H: slipe for transporting stones, turf, etc.: I: barrow slipe.

Fig 34

neighbour's trap and enjoying myself thoroughly; the fact that it was a fine day may have helped of course, because the trap was open to the elements and could be uncomfortable in wintertime.

One of the most interesting vehicles to travel on the roads in the old days was the gipsy vardo – or caravan as we refer to it today. Vardos were extremely colourful, and were an intrinsic part of early circuses. Tinkers and itinerants generally travelled in similarly shaped, but less colourful caravans.

Bicycles travelled the roads too from about 1900, although the hobby-horse and phantom bicycles were known before then. The boneshaker – an aptly named bicycle if ever there was one – did have pedals, but the rider had to pedal frantically to make even the slowest progress. As for the penny farthing – its main disadvantage was its high front wheel topped by the saddle; the pedals were also attached to the front wheel, and for a tall man the total diameter of the wheel, which could be five feet (about 1½m), was determined by his leg length and pedalling method. The diameter of the front wheel of a woman's bicycle was considerably less.

Lighting one's path was important when the roads were rutted and filled with potholes. In 1898 the first acetylene (carbide) lamp was designed for use with the bicycle and did wonders for night cycling. When my father was young and a keen cyclist he never went anywhere on the bike without his carbide lamp and bicycle-clips, a pair of metal open rings which held the flaps of wide trousers neatly against the leg to avoid accidents with the spokes of the wheels. A bicycle-pump too was carried at all times because the roughness of the country roads could puncture a tyre, and all cyclists were encouraged to carry a chain-box, some solution and patches for a fast puncture. A few blasts from the pump might be sufficient to keep a slow puncture from hampering travel.

The Sunday Mass and a monthly expedition to the local town for food supplies were often the only outings in a woman's life. In some parts of the country it was traditional to walk to Sunday Mass. Crowds of people would be seen making their way along the Mass-path. The children of course 'got up to divilmint' by tying *traithníns* of grass together to make foot traps – a childish prank that often had hilarious results!

Chapter 8

Springtime on the Land

Traditionally the feastday of Saint Brigid, February 1 marked the beginning of the farming year, and in olden times the farming family assembled in one of the fields to 'turn the sod'. This was an annual ritual accompanied by the reciting of certain prayers. And traditionally, ploughing did not take place until that very important first sod had been turned by the spade. However, in recent times the ploughing often took place during the wintertime, usually before heavy frost.

THE PLOUGH

From the time of the primitive digging-stick, whether pointed or spade-like, people have tried to speed up the process of tilling the land. One of the earliest foot-ploughs known on Irish land was the *cos-chrom* (translated as 'bent-foot', meaning that one had to bend over when using it). For centuries the cumbersome breast-plough was used for opening the soil. A misnomer if there ever was one, the breast-plough was thrust forward with hip or thigh power rather than by the force of breast movements. In Ireland the heavy loy (from *laí* or *laighe*) was well known in parts of Cavan and its surrounding counties, and in the south west. It was said that a dozen strong men armed with loys could turn an acre in a day.

Footrests were important on digging implements; sometimes nothing more than a block of wood wedged into a socket at the side of the spade-head, sometimes incorporated in the original design of the piece of metal forming the head, they varied according to local preference. Size and shape of both footrest and digging-head were determined by local conditions, and were standardised in any one area. Swallow-tail blades and tapered blades were popular in some areas, whilst straight blades, well sharpened, were the norm elsewhere. In Mayo the gowl-gob (from *gabhal-gob*, meaning forked beak) was a curious two-headed spade used in loose sandy soil, where it was said to be ideal for making ridges.

The Irish spade differed from the English not only in its narrow bent blade, but also in other respects, such as the way it was put to use – the Irish dig with the right foot, the English with the left!

The early ploughs were primitive implements, even the early versions of the modern plough. With many of the early wooden ploughs used in Ireland an implement called a mattock, or *matóg*, was used to turn the first layer of earth. It was a sort of hoe and was difficult to use over a long period. The first real improvements in the development of the plough occurred in the 1700s, with the first lightweight plough arriving into the British Isles from Holland. However, it was a Scotsman named James Small who invented a plough which one could operate easily whilst keeping the horses under control without the assistance of a second person. The first all-iron plough was built in 1800, and since then ploughs of all shapes, sizes and capabilities emerged annually. A trip to any folk museum – the Johnstown Castle farm museum in Wexford in particular – will vouch for this. And you will find that no two ploughs will be exactly the same, even though there were hundreds of each type made.

There were swing ploughs and wheel ploughs. The turnwrest plough had two blades and was simply turned around at the end of each furrow to make the return trip using the other blade, and it could be either swing or wheel. Generally, swing ploughs had no wheels and were popular with small farmers because they were cheap to buy. Because they sometimes had a wooden frame, few have survived.

The multi-furrowed plough was introduced before the end of the 1880s and was a great improvement for the farmer with the big acreage, for it meant that he could get a lot of ploughing done in a relatively short time. However, it was a very heavy implement in the early stages of its development and required far too many horses to pull it, and therefore didn't enjoy too much success. The two-furrow plough was much more successful, at least until the advent of steam, when the steam tractors pulled the multi-furrowed plough with considerable ease.

When ploughing for tillage the most suitable length for a furrow was 220-250 yards, and it was from this that the old division of the mile – the furlong (furrow-in-length) – evolved. The time taken to turn the horses at the ends of the furrows added up significantly, so

---

Figure 35   A: early Irish foot-plough; B: using a breast-plough; C: the gowl-gob; D: clay shovel; E: thigh pads worn by user of breast-plough; F: *cos chrom* plough; G: pair of plough-spanners; H: early swing plough; I: wooden frame harrow; J: dragboard (County Kerry); K: clod-breaker; L: metal earth-roller; M: levelling box in use; N: breast-plough; O: homemade clod-breaking machine; P: spring harrow.

Fig 35

that in a field with fifty turns to the acre a full thirty minutes or more were taken up with the turning. Two horses were usual, although as many as six were employed where land was particularly heavy. The average speed was 2 m.p.h. In a day a man and his horses walked up to eight or nine miles, and in the case of two horses, each one pulled a weight of up to 280lbs.

Steam power in the 1920s brought considerable changes. Following experimentation, it was discovered that the ploughing was a greater success if two machines were used together, which meant that only tillage contractors, as they called themselves, could afford to do steam ploughing. They travelled from farmer to farmer, quickly earning the cost of their new machinery. But it wasn't always a great success; the power of the steam engines drove the plough very deep, sending the valuable top soil too far down, which was detrimental to subsequent crops in the case of thin soil.

The success of two engines working together depended on a rapport between the two engine-men, for the only means of communication during a ploughing session was the engine whistle, which they blew loudly in various signals to 'voice' their messages. The whistles didn't carry well on windy days, and this often meant that the work had to stop. A six-furrow plough could work up to fourteen acres in a day, which compared rather well with the one acre ploughed by horse-power.

THE PARTS OF THE PLOUGH

Early ploughs were simple in structure, but the more recent creations were complicated pieces of machinery. The share was the cutting part of the implement, and on early ploughs which were invariably wooden with only one share, they were known as winding-boards. When iron shares were used, several interchangeable shares were used on the one plough, and their cutting angle could be altered. The coulter (*coltar*) made the vertical cut into the soil immediately in front of the share. Continuing behind the share was the mouldboard which was the most prominent part of the implement.

A wheel could easily be clogged up with clay and be difficult to pull. A sharp object was used to remove the clay; alternatively, a pair of special wheel-scrapers was attached to the plough. A spanner, too, was necessary on occasion and was carried in a special socket. Chain-traces were the chains by which the horses pulled the plough. They were kept clear of the animal's body by means of a cross-bar called a whippletree or swingletree, or by the doubletree in the case of two or more horses. These attachments were fashioned from ash wood with iron grips, but special all-iron or all-steel ones were used for very heavy work.

The earth which was drawn back into furrows by the plough had to be broken up before the seeds could be sown. Clod-breaking implements were fashioned to do this, including extra-heavy mallets. However, machines such as grubbers and the cultivator appeared during the early 1900s and did a very efficient job – six acres could be broken up in a single day. A grubbing-hoe was a special implement used for this purpose in parts of the west and south.

When the clods were broken, a roller was drawn over them to flatten down the earth even more. Rollers varied in design from lightweight wooden ones which had to be drawn over the ground many times to give decent results, to heavyweight metal 'Cambridge' rollers for extra heavy work with more than one or two horses. The drag-board was used in poorer areas, especially in Kerry and the west.

The harrowing was the next job. This was accomplished with the toothed harrow which was drawn over the rolled ground to rough it and make it suitable for seeding. Harrows varied from homemade wooden frame harrows with curved wooden or iron tines (teeth), to multiple disc harrows and spring-tooth harrows. Chain harrows were also known, and often came in zig-zag patterns for well-dispersed work.

The more advanced harrows were driven, which meant that the operator could control both machine and horses from a bucket-like seat. Like the plough, the primitive harrow is of great antiquity, and has appeared in many illuminated manuscripts, including the Bayeaux Tapestry of 1080.

SOWING THE GRAIN

The next job in the tillage field was the sowing of the grain. I can remember seeing my father hand-sowing from a scooped-up apron held before him. He had never invested in a proper sowing-fiddle, which was a small machine which sent seed broadcast when the 'bow' was moved over and back rhythmically. The seed was held in a sack inside the seed-box of the machine and a measured amount was released with each movement of the bow, expelling it for anything up to twelve feet (3.5m or so), which meant that less walking was necessary than with the apron, or its alternative the seed-basket or seed-hip. The single-wheel, barrowlike broadcaster was also used; it was wheeled along by hand, its long wooden hopper having apertures on the underside for releasing the seeds evenly, which were sent broadcast by little brushes arranged along the hopper. On big farms where huge fields were seeded, the horse-drawn broadcaster was used. When in use the two seed boxes were arranged in line and the axle and gear wheels at each end provided the power for the internal mechanism which sent the seed forth in measured amounts.

The swivel broadcaster was a large horse-drawn affair, introduced as the 'new improved' broadcasting machine, and it cost no more than £13 to buy! It had only one seed-box, lined with zinc at the bottom, which sent the seeds through to the ground. The box was centred on the main shaft of the vehicle and therefore placed no extra weight on the horse's back. However, some boxes were as wide as sixteen feet (almost 5m), and could not pass through gateways when in the open position. So, to close them, the farmer moved a lever which swivelled them on the main frame and they closed over so that one end was directly behind the horse's tail and the other beyond the main body of the vehicle.

Once the seed was sown, a second harrowing was advisable to roughen up the ground and bury at least half of the grains at a gentle depth below surface level. The roller or a levelling-box was then employed to smooth the ground, and a scarecrow (*taibhse*) was erected to keep the crows away. Other crow-scaring devices were introduced, but the *taibhse* was traditional, and was a good way of using old clothes. Clappers, consisting of two boards lightly tied by cords to each side of a third board with a handle at the end, were rattled to frighten the crows away; using clappers meant that the farmer or one of his children had to be in the vicinity of the tillage field at all times throughout the day. Nor is the modern 'banger', as we call it locally, a modern phenomenon, as some people might expect. This method of scaring crows was developed as long ago as 1850. My father recalls how one particular 'bang' method worked. In the old days carbide (acetylene) for the lamps was bought in a tin, but the tin was not discarded when empty. Instead, my grandfather kept it until springtime, when he punctured a hole at the base and placed in it a small piece of grey-white carbide. A drop of water, often some spittle, was aimed at it to rise the acetylene gas, and the lid was secured as tightly as possible. A match was then struck close to the hole, whilst the striker held his head well away. Too light a lid caused a blaze to shoot forward, but if it was properly secured, a loud bang reverberated around the field and sent the troublesome crows squawking for the nearest cover.

The rook-battery was another creator of noise. It consisted of a

---

Figure 36   A-E: single dibbers; F: multiple dibber; G: seed-hip; H: seed-box with shoulder-strap; I: seed-box with hand-grasp; J-L: potato-planters; M: sowing-fiddle; N-Q: bird-scaring devices; R: using the sowing-fiddle; S: bean-barrow; T: sowing corn from a hip-basket; U: sowing-fiddle; V: the 'new improved' sowing-machine of the 1800s.

Fig 36

circular plate of tin eighteen inches in diameter with a strong hoop soldered onto the circumference. Twenty-four or so embrasures were pierced into the hoop, and at each of these a small brass cannon was mounted, and all were loaded with gunpowder. A solution of saltpetre providing the firing power – a cotton wire was dipped into it and then held onto the touch-hole of each cannon by copper wire attached to the platform. The battery stood in the cornfield on three legs, and was moved regularly so the rooks and other crows wouldn't get used to having the sound come at them from one direction only.

OTHER CROPS

The 'spud', or potato was the most important root crop, and remains so for most of us even today in rural areas. Nowadays we eat Golden Wonders and Kerr's Pinks with relish, but in the old days the popular strains were Epicure, Red Elephant and Champion, whilst Aran Banners were fed to the pigs.

My father plants potatoes just as his father before him did – in lazybeds. These were wide seed-drills separated from each other by narrow trenches. The bank of earth which formed the actual ridge was about three feet (1m) in width (three stalks wide). The seeds, which were cut in half with part of an 'eye' remaining in each half, were sown in March-April, and the young foliage was visible in May. However, the crop wasn't ready for the first harvesting until late July at the earliest.

The dibber, or dibble, was the traditional planting tool. It was used to make holes for the seed, which were planted directly from a large *ciséan* (basket), one by one. In parts of Cavan and the midlands the dibber was known as the 'steeveen' (from the Irish *stibhín*) and was always used by the woman of the house, who was said to be 'guggering' (from *gogaire*, meaning to make holes for spuds).

'Earthing-up' or *lánú* of the potatoes was done twice in the course of the following months – three weeks after the actual sowing, and again a month later when the stalks were well out of the ground. In the midlands the shovel was used to scoop up loose clay from the trench and distribute it over the ridge. In the south and west the plough was drawn between the ridges, which were traditionally wider there, to break the earth for the same kind of earthing-up. The spraying against blight was done before the blossoms appeared. A solution of bluestone and washing-soda was prepared in the kitchen and taken to the potato field, where the farmer commenced spraying with a besom by dipping it into the solution and jerking it away from him so that liquid was sent broadcast. The smell of blight was often detected in the month of August, but if it was detected earlier, before the crop was yet edible, fear was struck in the farmer's heart. In 1845, it was said to have been detected in most areas as early as June.

The turnip was another important rural crop. It was sown in long drills, often running the length of the field alongside the potato ridges. The tiny seeds were treated with red lead prior to sowing, as a guard against birds taking them, and they were sometimes sown with a special seed-hopper or drill. Less well-off farmers had seed barrows, and the poorest farmers simply sowed by hand. As the crop advanced towards maturity a lot of weeding was necessary, and this too was done by hand, using a hoe of some kind in the early stages, and only the hands for the thinning out stage, when eight out of every ten plants were removed from the drill to allow the remaining two to grow well.

The hand-hoe was replaced on the larger farms by horse-drawn hoes, drawn between two rows each time. A pair of tines on each side removed the weeds from the inner edges of the drills, but did not damage the turnip plants. Experience taught the farmer how to gauge the distance between drills when making them in the first place.

THE BOG IN SPRINGTIME

Peatland covered a good percentage of rural Ireland, and in the old days almost every farmer had a *portach,* or bank of peat to work on in the spring. The bog was a lonely wilderness, whose size was determined by its location. In Donegal, for instance, the bogs and moors seemed to stretch on for ever, whereas in the midlands a bog was often a stretch of acid ground running along a river valley, with verdant hills and even buildings visible from its deepest depths. I loved the bog when I was young and have many pleasant memories of hours spent exploring amongst the bulrushes and unusual grasses which lined the fast-flowing freshwater streams criss-crossing it. A variety of sights and sounds indigenous to that particular environment became familiar to me over the years – the goatlike call of the jacksnipe, the lonesome whine of the curlew, the shriek of the otter, and the distinctive bark of the fox in the early evening. The most awesome sight has to be 'Jack the Lantern', a huge ball of gas which rose from the ground and floated by in all its glowing glory! The water from the bog streams was always crystal-clear and lovely to drink, and watercress flourished in great abundance.

My grandfather's midland bog produced a dark peat which dried rock-hard, but in other parts of the country the peat remained brown to grey-brown, depending on the type of bog. A bog which was *trom fhódach* was heavy-sodded ground, and a *portach dhá fhód deag* was particularly good because it was 'twelve-sod-deep'. Where a farmer didn't own a bog of his own, he could lease 'a bit of a digging' from the

State. This, of course, was often a risk in damp years because turf needed a 'keen breeze' to dry it for use in the fire.

A whiff of pale grey turfsmoke escaping from where the 'tay' brewed in the old black kettle was often the only indication to the passer-by that the bog was peopled. It was traditional in the old days for a large group of men from an area to work at each man's turf in turn, each one playing host when his turf was being harvested. One season's cutting supplied a family with firing for the year – the black bottom-peat for the winter use, the brown sphaghnum peat for the summer use.

When cutting peat, the first stage was the opening up of the bank, which involved the removal of the top layer of tough, fibrous peat referred to as 'fum'. It made poor firing, but a slipe-load of these parings was a welcome sight to a poor man with no peat of his own. A flatcher was used to remove the parings from the bog; a common garden spade worked equally well in recent times. Soft dry parings were sometimes kept back to be spread out on the cutaway bog below the bank as dry footing.

When cutting turf it was very important for the *sleadóir* (turf-cutter) to 'keep a straight face' – that is to keep a straight face on the bank being worked. A man who couldn't was called a 'clod cutter' and was derided by his mates. Later, when finishing off, it was customary in some north western areas to leave three steps of turf uncut. This was to avoid the curse of Saint Columcille, who was once trapped in a boghole, and subsequently put a curse on any turf-cutter who didn't leave a way out of the hole.

The traditional turf-cutting implement was the slane (also shlawn, from *slèan*). Generally the type of slane was determined by the type of bog being worked, and by the method of turf-cutting. Basically, there were two methods – vertical and horizontal – though each farmer had his own favourite way of thrusting the slane or lifting the turves from the bank.

Vertical cutting, or underfooting, was favoured in thin, upland bogs and was difficult work, whereas horizontal cutting, or breasting, was the easier method used in lowland bogs. With breasting there was considerably less strain on the back, and the work was fairly fast because the turf-cutter put the sods directly from the slane on to the barrow.

Figure 37   A: bog-hatchet; B: bog-barrow; C: trying-iron, used for locating buried timber; D: turf-pick; E: turf-cutter of British origin; F-K: turf-cutters and slanes; L: poor woman bringing home the turf; M: using donkey to transport turf; N: bog wheelbarrow; O: three types of slane – south, midlands and north respectively; P: hand-barrow.

Fig 37

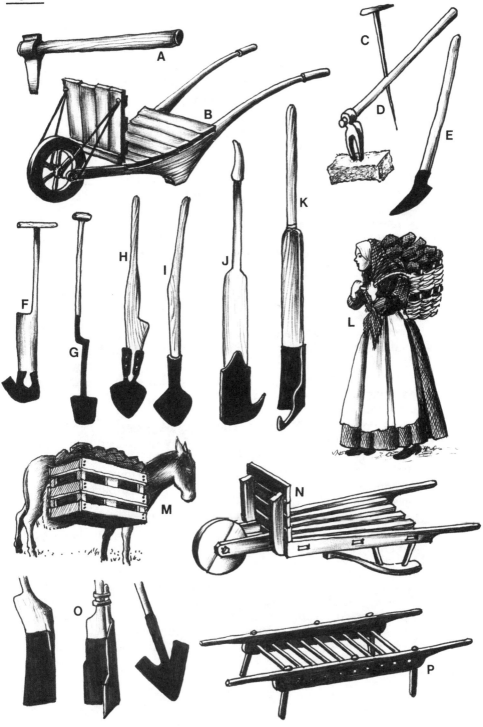

Slanes were made to measure and varied quite a bit in size and design. Consisting of four parts – the blade (*iarann*), the spade-tree (*sail*), the shaft (*cos*) and the hilt (*dorn*) – the slane is a very old implement. The breasting implement was distinguished from the underfooting slane by the upward slant of its cutting edge, whereas the wing of the underfooter slanted downwards. Sometimes some tow roots got caught up on the blade and made working difficult.

The bog-barrow was an important means of transportation in the bog. Fashioned from laths of wood (often crudely, and without any wheel at all), it helped to transfer the freshly-cut sods of turf from the bank to the drying ground. Sometimes a small slipe was used, especially on wet ground, where it could be pulled along the slithery surface more easily than a barrow would have been wheeled or carried.

The drying of the turf took a long time, especially in wet years. Sometimes the whole harvest was lost, but when it wasn't inclement the sodden turves were removed from the barrow and spread on the *scair* by a spreader, using a turf-fork or pike. A week later, following a fairly dry spell, the turves were ready for footing. Six to eight turves were placed against each other in sets of two, more along the top, to form a *coirceog* (cone-shaped mound). The number of *coirceogs* depended on the amount of turf being footed. Footing was generally children's work, done after school or on a fine Saturday, and my father recalls how it used to be when boredom set in as the work became routine towards the end of the session – one remark of an insulting or scathing nature was enough to spark off a session of scraw-flinging, which all too easily went beyond the realms of fun. It wasn't unusual for someone to end up in a boghole!

Once the turf was declared 'bone dry' by the farmer it was built into a large rick and covered with a water-resistant roof of thatch. However, by now the wind should have formed a tough, waterproof skin on the sods and drained them of most of their 80% moisture. Once the turf was sufficiently 'seasoned' in the autumn, it was drawn home to the farmyard for storing. A donkey and cart provided the usual transport in the midlands, but in the west and south, slide-cars and creels were used for this important end-of-year task.

Figure 38   A: removing 'top dressing' dung from tip-cart; B: dung-knife; C:cow-pat spreader; D: dung-drag; E: graip; F: smith-made dung-lifter; G: two-prong dung-drag; H:cow-pat lifter; I: dowelled dung-fork (home-made); J: serrated dung-knife; K: dung-drag; L: dung-fork with holding hooks on prongs; M: liquid manure-spreader; N: old fashioned hay-baler.

Fig 38

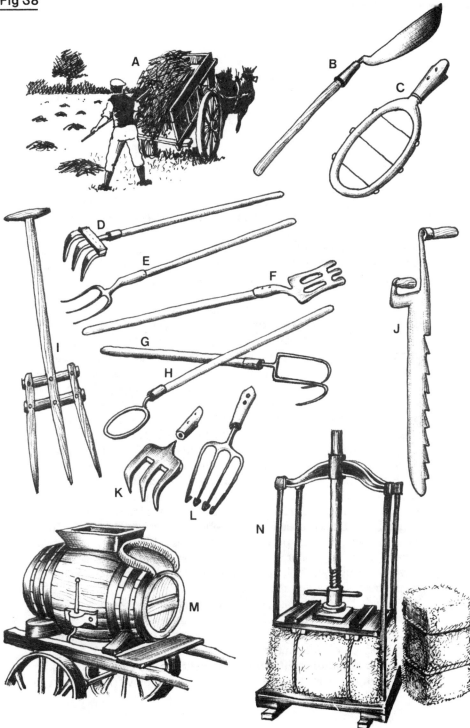

Chapter 9

The Harvest

The work-period known as the harvest spanned the summer and autumn months, starting with the haymaking and concluding with the Harvest Home festivities. Compared to modern harvesting, it was slow and tedious work in the old days, rushed only when rain was expected; and in those days farmers used their knowledge of the countryside and nature as their weather guide.

THE HAYMAKING

Preparation for the haymaking was made as early as February, when the farmer set aside one or more fields for meadow. Then, later in the spring, he set about encouraging the crop to produce a higher yield by spreading farmyard manure on the still pasture-quality grass. This spreading of manure was known as top-dressing, and was accomplished in one of four ways. Firstly, it could be spread as a solid, direct from the dungheap in the yard. The well-to-do farmers often had carts with tilting mechanisms which made the removal of the dung onto the field a fairly simple process. But I can remember seeing my father use a pitchfork to remove the dung from his cart, a little at a time until the selected field was dotted with small blackish heaps. Later it was spread out evenly until the whole field was dressed. Some farmers had a dung-drag, a special fork for pulling the dung from the cart onto the ground. And a wooden dung-fork, pegged together with dowels, was often used instead of a graip to spread it. In very poor areas manure spreading often meant lifting cowpats from one field and putting them on another, using an implement with a circular head.

Liquid fertiliser was sometimes used in preference to solid farmyard manure. A barrel distributor mounted on two wheels and drawn by a horse was used for dispersing the liquid (urine collected over a period of time in the sheds). An early form of muck-spreader, or 'box distributor' as it was called in early catalogues, was used by well-to-do farmers to spread soft slurry manure by spraying it onto

118

the land. The manure fell from a transverse box-like hopper onto revolving tines which then flung it from the rear of the machine.

The fourth method of manuring land was to fill a seed-hopper with bone-meal and distribute it evenly on the ground, a method used in the east and north when farmyard manure wasn't produced in the amounts required.

Once the meadow was tall enough – usually mid June – the farmer arranged to have it cut. If he didn't have a scythe or – in recent times – a mowing machine he had a neighbour or contractor do the mowing for him. Different types of grasses were known – the *féar caorach* was the sheep's fescue, the *féar capaill* was the timothy grass, and the *féar garbh* was the cocksfoot, which produced a particularly coarse type of hay. A bad grass was *féar gaoil*, the quitch grass, and the *féar gorta* was the 'hungry' grass, a type of mountain grass which brought on an unnatural craving for food if one should inadvertently step on it! The 'cure' was a little food – as little as a crumb even – carried on one's person!

When the hay was cut into swaths it was left to dry for a couple of days, then turned by fork or graip for drying on the other side. It was then shaken out and made into *cociní* (cockeens, cutyeens or lapcocks) and, unless very dry, left to stand in the field for some days for further drying. Lap-cocks varied from rolls like ladies' muffs, through which the wind breezed, to small cocks. Once fully dry they were shaken out for a second time and built into proper field-cocks between seven and eight feet tall. *Súgáns*, or hayropes, were then twisted and drawn over the cocks to secure them. Heavy stone weights at the ends of the ropes held them down in high wind. The farmer usually 'headed' the cocks at this stage too. This was done by raking all the loose hay from the cock to tidy it, then replacing it on top with a pitchfork. The best time for cutting hay was in June when the grasses were in flower; a crop of hay from a June cutting was a prized possession. Also, it left behind a significant 'eddish' (aftergrass).

The mowing-machine was introduced at the turn of the century, but prior to the machine age, the scythe was the traditional hay-cutting implement. And even today it is hard to beat it for mowing awkward gardens and corners of fields. The long-handled scythe has always been favoured by Irish farmers, and because it was built to the farmer's own specifications in the old days, no two scythes were exactly the same.

Basically, the scythe was made up of four important parts – the handle, the handgrips, the blade and the guard.

A smith-made blade was a prized possession, and old blades were never thrown away, but instead were hafted for slicing vegetables, or for slicing hard-packed hay from the haggard rick, and for a variety of other farmyard cutting jobs. The blade was sharpened with a special honing-stone called a strickle, a job which was repeated often during a mowing session. The strickle was carried in a leather sheath attached to the farmer's belt, or placed in a special socket on the handle of the implement. An older method of sharpening was with the riff, which was fashioned from wood instead of the more familiar stone, smeared with goose grease at the sharpening end, and then sanded. When pulled over the blade in one direction only it acted like a file. Coarse sand was used when a slightly serrated edge for cutting briars or tough weeds was required, fine sand for field work.

The handle of the scythe was called the *crann*, the *snáith*, or the sned, depending on the part of the country. The average length was five and a half feet, and a curve was general, although straight-handled scythes were known in certain areas.

When honing the blade or fixing the headgrips the farmer held the scythe upright to avoid accidents, for a scythe balanced wrongly could easily topple over and do him an injury. A metal spike at the end of the *crann* usually solved the problem by securing the implement on the ground. The spike was called a grass-nail.

The cradle was a feature of scythes used by farmers with small crops of meadow, or by farmers who cut the odd swath when required. The cradle collected the hay neatly, leaving no gathering following cutting. Another type of cradle was used for carrying hay uphill. Generally homemade, it varied greatly in design, but the principle was the same (Figure 41E).

The horse-drawn mowing machine was a riding machine with a sprung seat and a long draught pole centred between two horses. It travelled on two sizeable landwheels, set wide apart and slatted for better grip. Consisting of three main parts – the truck or carriage (main body), the cutting blade and bar, and the draught-pole and whipple-tree for attachment to the harness – the mowing-machine was at its best when brand new and with a sharp blade. However it became sluggish very quickly, so that the blades required constant sharpening and altering.

The actual haymaking didn't really begin until the swaths were on the ground. The hand tools used included the fork, the rake and the four-pronged graip. A variation of the field-rake which was worked by the women, was the drag-rake. This was a much larger implement and was always worked by the farmer himself.

Figure 39 A: using a scythe; B: drag-rake; C: horse-drawn mowing-machine; D: hand-rake; E: using the hand-rake; F: side delivery rake; G: drag-rake; H: scythe with cradle for grass; I: scythe with temporary cradle for corn; J: corn-scythe; K-L: blade honing-strickle; M: tedding-machine; N: paddy-rake.

Fig 39

Some of the haymaking machinery was dangerous. For instance the tedding machine had projecting tines which lay open and unprotected on many of the earlier machines; a few had a protective covering of iron sheeting, but accidents involving children occurred all too frequently. The 'tedder' teased the hay into the cocking stage, and a horse-drawn machine rake, known as a dump-rake, was then used to bring the hay close to where it was to be built into a cock. Another machine, used in the drying stage, was the swath-turner, which saved a lot of time in the early stages of haymaking. The side-delivery rake sometimes assisted it by drawing every two freshly-turned swaths into one windrow.

The field cocks stood in the field for anything up to two months, then had to be drawn home to the haggard, the traditional storing place for the crops. The hay was transported to the haggard in fine autumn weather usually in the hay-bogy in the midlands. Other bogys, sometimes called sweeps, were also known. Horse-drawn hay-carts – some with a hay-rack fitted – and slide-cars were also used, and in very poor regions a donkey might be seen being led home with a mighty burden of hay on his back.

Some of my clearest childhood memories are of helping my father bring home the hay. My contribution to the actual work was minimal – mostly because I kept diverting from course to help myself to blackberries which flourished so abundantly in the hedges – but I remember being given the job of driving the donkey and hay-filled cart from the field to the haggard where my father added my load to the growing rick.

I can also remember helping my father make hay-ropes the old way, using a homemade winder, fashioned from a length of twisted wire. Sometimes rope-winders were made from wood, and were called thraw-hooks, or from a mixture of wood and wire and called scud-winders. The ropes, or *súgáns* as they were called, were made by feeding the hay slowly onto the hook of the winder, which was constantly turned. The *rópadóir* (twister) moved away as the length of the rope increased. The footrope was the name given to the rope securing a large haycock.

The hay in the haggard was built into a large rick. Well-to-do farmers often had special elevators to take the hay up to the rick as it was growing. But generally, men on the ground pitched the hay up to men on the top, and when the rick was made, a ladder was provided. Then the sides of the rick were manicured with a rake, especially at

Figure 40 A: rope-twister; B: bringing home the hay on hay-bogy; C: hay-sweep; D: child's homemade fork; E: large hay-scythe; F-K: hay-rope twisting tools; L: loading up the hay for the journey to the haggard.

Fig 40

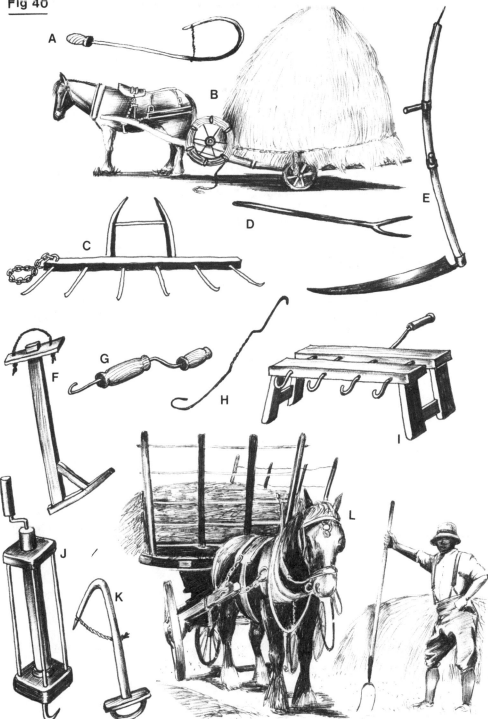

A

B

C

D

E

F

G

H

I

J

K

L

the base, and headed, then secured with strong ropes from which rocks were suspended. Once the cold biting winds of winter came the hay in the haggard was used as fodder, and was a vital food source for the animals in the fields.

THE GOLDEN HARVEST

The 'Golden Harvest' began with the preparation of the soil as outlined in Chapter 8, and ended with the Harvest Home festival. Strictly speaking, though, it began in August when the ripe corn was golden yellow.

There were four main corn crops – wheat, oats, barley and rye. In the midlands, oats and barley were the main crops, in the east wheat, in the west and south oats and barley, and in the north oats and rye, and also flax, which was a flowering plant grown as the raw material in the linen industry.

Spring wheat was sown in March, together with any other cereal crops to be harvested during the summer. Winter wheat was sown later in the year. Oats was the most common crop, mainly because the damp climate suited it so well and the straw was extremely versatile. However, with oats the harvesting had to be well gauged because overripe grains invariably fell to earth and were lost during the cutting. With all of the cereal crops such 'lodging' was a risk in stormy weather, when the wind beat relentlessly at the waving corn and sent some of it to ground level, rendering it impossible to cut. Badgers and flocks of birds also had the same damaging effect.

The sickle is one of the oldest surviving implements in farming, and indeed it is still used in areas inaccessible to the reaping machine. The design of the sickle is outstanding because one can use it for a whole day without feeling unduly tired. Traditionally, women reaped with the sickle and men with the heavier toothed reaper, a sort of sickle with a heavier blade and serrated edge. The corn was cut by bending over it, grasping a bunch of straw in the left hand, inserting the hook and drawing it towards the body in a sawing action. Gentleness was important if no grain was to be lost in ripe crops. It was also important to cut 'low and clean – to the living earth', as they used to say in the midlands years ago.

Loghter-hooks (from *luchtar*, 'armful') or pick-thanks drew the loghters into sheaves. Resembling a walking-stick, the loghter-hook was a 'tidy' of sorts, keeping the corn neat. A gavel was a similar

---

Figure 41 A: early mowing-machine; B-D: mowing-sickles; E: hay and straw cradle, used for carrying small loads uphill on the back; F: barley-gavel; G: straw-fork; H: barley-fork (rare); I-K: mowing-sickles; L: homemade gavel; M: scutching flax; N: at the flax dam.

Fig 41

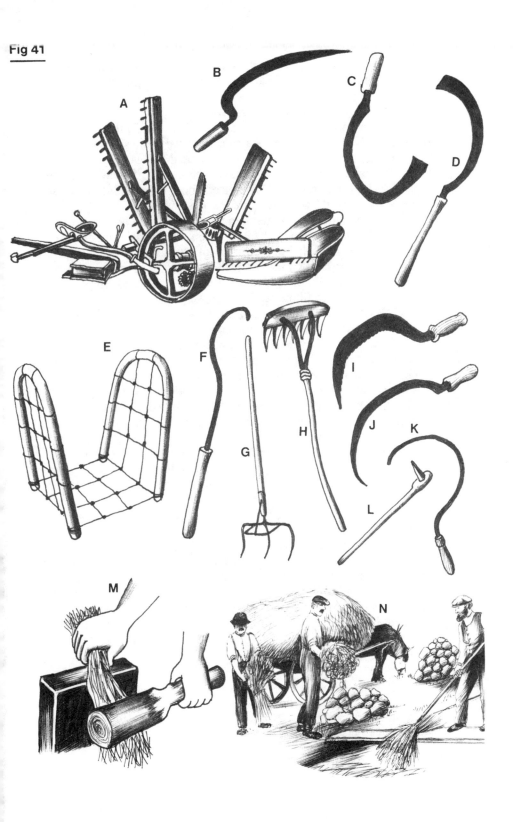

crooked implement used with barley, whose seed-heads were inclined to take up a lot of space and required more control from the reaper.

Once the loghters were bound into sheaves, a few more workers came behind and arranged the sheaves into stooks. In the midlands, stooks were built up in stages, starting with five or six sheaves for the first drying, then ten or twelve, with a head of two sheaves. The tiebands, made with a length of straw deftly twisted away from the sheaf, was loose enough to allow a toe of a boot to fit easily. Too loose and the sheaf would collapse with the least handling.

Wind and sun dried and seasoned the stooks over a period of a few weeks. Field-stacks then had to be made, and consisted of ten or twelve stooks with their butts out. Various local names were known, such as *adag* (north-east), *stucóg* (west) and 'bart' (south). In my own locality, the midlands, it was called a *síog,* pronounced 'shig'.

When the corn, as all the cereal crops were collectively known, was dry it was transported to the haggard in large carts. A large rick was built and for that job it was every man who was available! Two kinds of rick were built – the knee-stack, made by a man on top and a group of men on the ground pitching up the sheaves, and the over-hand stack, made from the ground without a ladder.

The *meitheal* was an important feast associated with the harvest. Originally the word *meitheal* was the Irish word for a gang of workmen working together with any major crop, but over the centuries it has come to mean 'Harvest Home', the all-important festival at the end of the summer when the harvest was in and the country folk celebrated their prosperity. The feasting at the *meitheal* was shameless, and there were barrels and half-barrels of 'porter' and 'stout', and the odd *cruiscín lán* filled with *póitín* and *uisce beatha*. Dancing and music generally prevailed and the evening was guaranteed to inspire gaiety.

The *meitheal* gradually became a thing of the past when mechanisation shortened the harvesting period. When the reaper-binder appeared it was received with a mixture of awe and disbelief, for not only could it cut the corn efficiently, but it could also bind it. Speed was improved and in some cases, quality. When the massive combine-harvester appeared on the scene it did everything and in a very short time, thus eliminating harvest-time as our grandparents knew it.

Figure 42 A: sheaf of corn; B: stook of sheaves; C: small haggard stack on platform; D: reaper-binder; E: straw-knife; F: haggard platform, used in areas liable to flooding; G: harvest scene in the field.

Fig 42

THE FLAX HARVEST

Flax harvesting was more common in the northern counties than in any other part of Ireland, although some considerable flax crops were grown in isolated pockets in the south. When grown for fibre it was harvested directly after the powder-blue blooms wilted but before the flower-heads had produced seeds. The tall stalks were either harvested at the ground or pulled by the roots, and from then on were referred to as lint. Teams of farmers worked together at the flax harvesting and were known as boons. The work was particularly tough – virtually impossible for a beginner – because the tough fibrous plants were extremely hard on the hands, causing blistering and welts, and the continuous stooping was back-breaking. A sheaf of stalks was called a beet and contained three or four handfuls, usually bound with rushes. They were loaded onto a cart and taken to the lint-hole for steeping, or dubbing as it was sometimes called, so that the stalks could ret for a period of up to ten days. Peaty water was best and when the flax was sufficiently retted a foul odour permeated the surroundings. The beets were now slimy and ugly and difficult to handle. However, once they were grassed on the green bank above the hole, they quickly dried out. Grassing was a skilled job, for individual stalks were not allowed to touch and dry into each other. Once dried, the stalks were tied into beets for a second time and carted to the bleaching-green or yard.

When the bleaching was completed the beets were built into stook-like gaits for the final seasoning. It was soon ready for scutching, the beating which tenderised the tough stalks.

THE THRESHING

Although the harvest officially came to an end with the *meitheal* in October, many farmers worked further with the corn in wintertime. Winnowing, threshing and milling were the three winter jobs which in former times were accomplished at intervals when the weather was suitable. In latter times the travelling mill combined two or more jobs during a brief visit.

The earliest method of threshing was done with the flail (stick-and-a-half). First of all the corn was removed from the stack and the sheaves torn open with the toe of a boot. On primitive farms where even a flail was a luxury the farmer scutched the corn by the handful

---

Figure 43   A: scutching corn (Aran Islands); B: winnowing, using a tray; C: two-man thresher; D: winnowing-basket; E: winnowing-machine; F: drum winnowing-machine; G: threshing-frame; H: scutching-pole; I: using the quern to grind corn; J-N: various flail hangings.

Fig 43

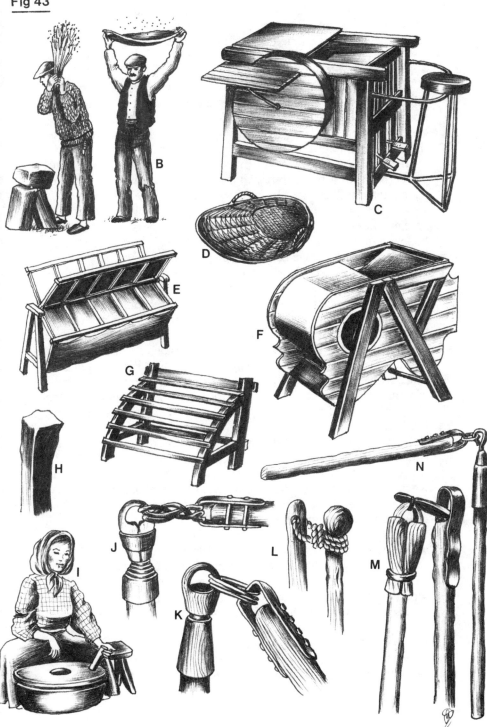

against a boulder or stout wooden post. The threshing-frame was an improvement on this. In parts of the west where they had very small crops the farmer scutched corn in the same way as flax farmers scutched flax so that the grain fell to the ground but the straw remained undamaged for thatching.

When I was young my father threshed with the flail which he'd inherited from his father. He spread a sheet on the barn floor and opened out a couple of sheaves at a time for beating. As the walloping got underway a steady rhythm developed, and he maintains it was the rhythm which kept him going later on when he was feeling tired.

In earlier times the favourite threshing place was the kitchen floor, preferably with a front and back door open to create a draught for taking the chaff away. The chaff was the lightweight corn husks which were separated from the corn proper during the beating. A special threshing board was kept by many farmers, who liked the hollow sound created when the flail was used on it, and a horse's skull buried close to the edge of the clay floor magnified the deep sound.

The flail consisted of three main parts – the handle, the mid-kipple or hanging, and the beater (swingle or soople). The handle was generally made from hazel and was $3\frac{1}{2}$ feet to 5 feet or so in length. In the midlands ashwood was sometimes used instead of hazel, but the beater was always fashioned from holly. The mid-kipple was made from anything pliable ranging from eelskin to rawhide. My grandfather used a thong of eelskin, which he drew between hoops of leather on each stick. In parts of Cavan, and the northern areas generally, a hole was bored through the handle and a groove through the beater. A similar method of tying was used in the west, using two holes instead of one.

When the threshing was completed the winnowing had to be done, and in former times a winnowing tray or riddle was used. The winnowing got rid of any remaining chaff and the best way to do this when using a tray or riddle was to stand on a stool or rock and shake the container vigorously in the wind above the head so that any chaff dislodged from the corn kernels would drift away in the breeze. A 'sweet' breeze was desired, even for the early winnowing machines which had sacking which flagged hard in the breeze.

The winnowing machine combined the jobs of threshing and winnowing in later models. The corn sheaves were fed into the drum, separated from the seeds inside and brought out at one end as straw. The seed came out at the other into sacks, and the chaff was blown

Figure 44 A: cotrel and jug; B: corn-scoop; C: sack-barrow; D: grain-shovel; E: threshing-mill; F: grain-shovel; G: straw-rake; H: scoop basket; I: barn rope-twister; J: bushel and strike; K: large steam-engine.

Fig 44

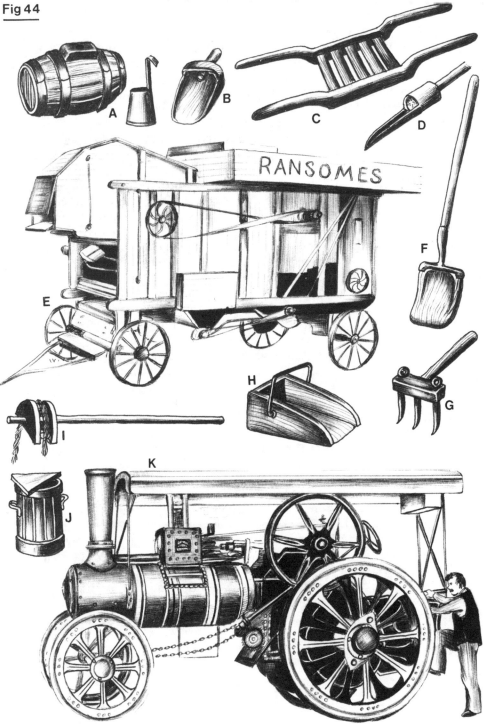

out from a separate channel to form a featherlight mound a short distance from the machine.

Large threshing mills adopted the same principle, but were much faster of course, and were generally powered by steam. There were many different models of threshing machines, winnowing machines and mills. The big mills worked on contract jobs only, but many farmers had small machines, such as hand-threshers and winnowing machines, which they loaned to neighbours.

The day of the threshing was a big day for the farmer when the mill and its attendant steam engine were expected, because it meant that a whole host of helpers came along too and required feeding at the end of the day. Young children were excited at the prospect for weeks and stared awestruck when the puffing monster with its shiny brass knobs and wheels came into the yard, together with the big mill. Once the fan belt was fixed and set in motion the mill slowly rocked into a humming rhythm and sent hens and turkeys scuttling away for cover. The work commenced and as the sheaves were opened and turfed into the depths of the machine the odd rat escaped and caused a minor panic amongst the men who pursued it relentlessly with pitchforks and any available missiles. And then as darkness fell the men trudged into the house with keen appetites and plenty of 'ould chat'.

The grain was carted to the local watermill, or ground at home within weeks of the threshing. In former times a quern was used to grind the corn. The quern is an ancient implement, consisting of two parts – the upper stone (which contained a hole and was sometimes referred to as a 'rocking stone' when found in a field by people who didn't know what it was and were inclined to associate it with the fairies) and the lower stone. The upper stone had a handle which was turned, bringing the stone with it over the seeds between the stones, thus crushing them. Querns were superseded by handmills and corn crushers and other small machines for home use.

The big mills were visited by the farmer with a decent harvest. He took a cartload of full sacks to his local miller and returned with sacks of flour and meal, the annual supply if the family wasn't a particularly large one. There were also a few windmills, a good example of which still stands (not operational) in Wexford today. Inside, the workings of both mills were the same – grindstones ground the corn, using the power of either water or wind. The flour when it emerged was quite warm after the milling process, and when baked in a cake was quite delicious.

Chapter 10

Homemade Things

Throughout the previous chapters I've described various things that farming households made, including kitchen furniture and modes of transport. Many of the things they made may seem very primitive by modern standards, but they served their purpose adequately, and often there wasn't anything to compare them with in any case. All kinds of material were worked into containers or tools, especially pliable materials which could be moulded, and wood. The tools which the farmer used for making things were invariably smith-made and simple, and occasionally a particularly gifted person could produce a work of art using very few tools.

Burden ropes were made and used for transporting small loads, such as a *brosna* of sticks or fodder. Larger loads, or loads of turf and finely-cut fodder which couldn't be carried by rope, were carried in *ciseáin* or wickerwork baskets. Some of these baskets had straps or strings for the shoulders.

Burden ropes were fashioned from all kinds of material – straw (for lightweights), hay, strands of tree bark and even seaweed. I can remember seeing my grandmother bringing rotting sticks she'd collected for the fire home on her back, using a modern rope in the old way. Just as ancient as the burden rope for the back was the *fáinnín* for the head. This was a ring of hay placed on the crown of the head to support considerable burdens such as a basket of laundry or turf.

Coastal people collected a lot of seaweed for making kelp, for manuring their infertile land and sometimes for food. And in the case of some islanders they had no carts or other large transporter to bring home a heavy load at a time, so they collected smaller loads in back-baskets, or in a pair of creels strapped to a donkey's back. On Aran, a sheepskin was tied to a person's back with a rope knotted at the front before the back-basket was fitted. When using creels the animal's back had to be protected too from the abrasive action of the hard wickerwork. Back-pads were made from straw or hay, or even from rushes. The pad was like a mat draped across the animal's back, and onto it was placed the straddle from which pins projected to take the handles of the creels. Tin panniers could also be attached, or wooden carrier boxes. I've seen good examples of pads and straddles in Knock Folk Museum.

The back-pad and straddle were sometimes joined together. Sometimes called the *cruit* (which means hump on the back), the combined pad and straddle were easy to put on. There were two types of straddle – the crook straddle and the split straddle. They each consisted of a pair of flat boards resting on a straw or hay mat as outlined above. The crook straddle had only one pair of boards from which hooks projected, the split straddle had two pairs, one smaller than the other. Osier (willow) ties reinforced the bridge between the larger ones, and in Kerry osier loops were sometimes used instead of creel hooks.

A belly-band held the straddle in position, with a supporting crupper running under the tail. A breast-band was added to the harness to balance the weight on the body when heavy burdens such as turf or hay were being transported. Straw ropes generally sufficed as belly-bands and cruppers but if possible the breast-band was fashioned from something stronger, such as leather. A simple bridle of twisted straw completed the harness.

Baskets were known by many different names, depending on their size and on the locality. A large basket was generally a *cliabh*, a fishing basket for holding nets was known as a *caiteog* in Antrim, and as a *ciseán* on the western seaboard. A *ciseog* was a shallow round basket, the type used for holding the potatoes on the table during mealtime and sometimes incorporating a small cup in the centre for salt. A *cleibhín* was a small basket, about the size of a modern bread-basket, and a *caitéog*, as well as being a fishing-basket in Antrim and a straw-rope, was also a plaited hen's nest and the name for the rush mats put on clay floors in the old days. In Clare any basket was referred to as a *lod*, and a *pana ciseán* was a badly-made basket, whereas a *cis* was a well-made wickerwork basket.

Basketmaking is one of the oldest crafts in the world and it is still a popular craft today. However, nowadays we weave wicker baskets for ornamentation in the home, but in the past basketmaking was a necessity. Many farmers had their own sally garden behind the house, and when the sallies were ready for harvesting they were cut

Figure 45 A: straw straddle; B: straw collar; C: two burden-ropes; D: panniers by horseback; E: belly-band; F: straw straddle; G: muzzle for calf; H: straw collar with wooden frame; I: creel-carrying straddle for donkey (a and b indicate hooks for creel support); J-K: ropemakers (see also Chapter 9, Figure 40).

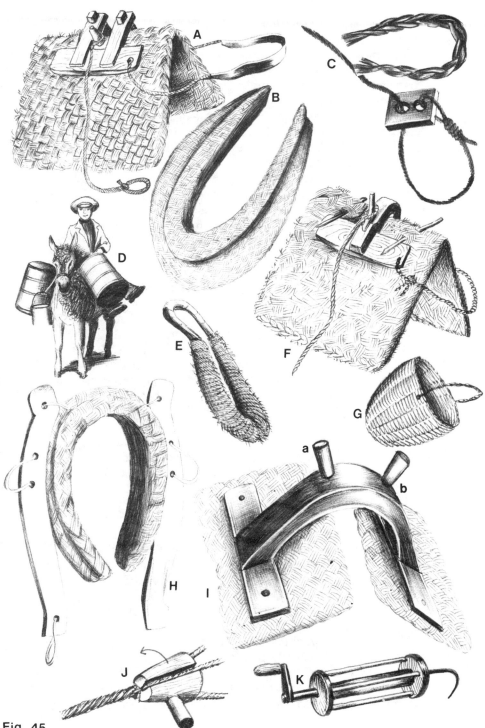

A

B

C

D

E

F

G

a

b

H

I

J

K

Fig 45

and arranged in bundles for private use or for sale on fairday.

The materials used in basketmaking included raffia (imported), cane (imported), willow, reed, rushes and sally, whilst rudimentary containers were woven from straw and hay. Basketmaking with sallies and willows was largely a male occupation because the work was hard on both skin and muscles. Adequate skill was acquired in less than a year by a youngster, and by the time he was in his thirties or forties and had a discerning eye, he could fashion a basket from memory using intricate work.

Two special baskets which required complicated work were the potato-skib, which was a wickerwork strainer (superseded by the colander) and the *sciathóg*, which was a special potato-basket for holding potatoes in the field during sowing. A *sciathóg* was also the name given to the detachable base of a creel.

The basketmaker who lent himself to all types of basketmaking needed to have a good selection of tools. A sharp billhook or knife was used for cutting and trimming, and various awls and bodkins for making holes. A small shears of some kind was used for nipping larger sticks. A good basketmaker cut and prepared his own rods, usually in the autumn when the crisp golden leaves were already shed. The rods were left for several weeks to season, then the rough-work rods were separated from those suited to fine weaving. The latter were stripped of their bark and soaked in hot water. They were naturally soft grey in colour, but could be dyed in various shades so that interesting effects could be achieved in the pattern. A well-dyed rod is said to have lasted for years without fading.

With willow the basketmaker had natural brown, natural fawn and natural white to choose from. They were not placed in water, but instead were stood upright against a wall or hedge once the bark was stripped off so that the damp stickiness could dry naturally.

The basketmaker usually worked sitting on a low plank of wood made of elm measuring three feet in length and two in width. It was raised a little above the ground at the back end and had a makeshift seat for comfort. The rods lay in a pile beside the craftsman as he worked. A special 'horse' – a sort of plank on legs over which one straddled just as if riding a horse – was used by craftsmen who made spale baskets (originally from Wiltshire, England) and trugs (of Lancashire origin). The bushel-trug was particularly useful for carrying potatoes and other produce on the land.

Nets and ropes, both thick straw *súgáns* and thin twines of twisted yarns, were an important part of daily life. Snared rabbits, for instance, were often brought home in nets, thatched roofs were covered with netting to keep the birds away, onions were stored in nets in wintertime, and nets were essential for fishing. Ropes tied down loads, carried loads as burden-ropes, held flapping trouser legs against the legs, and were moulded into makeshift baskets and mats. Netmaking was a skill known to all coastal fishermen. Certain knots were known – the sheet-bend, double-sheet bend and reef knot. Fishermen generally only used the first of these, using a thick needle and a 'lace', which was a short piece of wood. Not unlike hand-knitting, hand-netting followed moves such as casting on and casting off. The fibre used was sisal or hemp-twine.

Straw was woven into *súgán* seats (see Chapter 3), mats and various types of lightweight baskets. The craft of straw-weaving was known as lip-work. In Chapter 12 you can see how bee-skeps were woven; corn-bushels were constructed similarly. Straw plait was worked into hats, carrier-bags, and even door-panels when wood wasn't available locally. Originally, whole straws were used, but it was discovered that straw which was split gave a neater finish and also went further. Thraw-hooks and scud-winders like those shown in Chapter 9 were used to make the ropes. They were then twisted tightly in the direction the craftsmen desired until the object was complete.

One important use for straw was as a filler for horse-collars. In Figure 45 I've shown a whole straw collar, the type used originally without any covering. A piece of cloth was draped over the animal's neck before the collar was put on so as to avoid irritation to the animal's skin. Because of the wear and tear it was subjected to in the course of a day's work, the collar had to be replaced every so often. This meant that the farmer had to be proficient at making replacements as required.

Hens' nests were invariably fashioned from straw or rushes. The nesting-basket was always an attractive piece of workmanship, and was, apparently, made comfortable for more than economic reasons. Our ancestors, it would seem, believed that when the hens were squabbling amongst themselves at night before settling on their roosts, they were plotting to fly away from Ireland. A comfortable nesting-place and a warm hen-house were provided as a lure to keep them at home!

Different types of nesting-basket were known in different parts of the country. In the midlands the hens had to be content with wooden boxes lined with hay, and although they obliged the farmer's wife by laying in the carefully prepared boxes most of the time, they often wandered off in search of a sheltered bit of hedge or a convenient cavity in the hay-filled manger and laid their eggs there. The housewife always had to have her ear cocked for the sound of cackling from somewhere other than the hen-house.

In parts of the south west, county Limerick in particular, two- or three-tiered chicken-coops were the order of the day in most farmhouse kitchens; sometimes they were incorporated into the dresser. The coop was vacated and cleaned out during the day, and had fresh hay put in for the night when the hens were brought in from their farmyard wanderings. The coop was fashioned from wood with a slatted door at the front, and a good example may be seen in Bunratty Folk Park.

In parts of the west and far south the nesting-basket was suspended from a pole in the kitchen; sometimes as many as three or four separate nesting-baskets were provided, with the pole from which they were suspended serving as a roost at night. The alternative to a set of individual nesting baskets was a basket-box containing up to four or even six nesting-compartments.

For toolmaking, wood was widely utilised in the midlands, east and south where it was easily acquired. The most basic of kitchen tools, such as pounding-mallets and beetles were fashioned from a single length of solid wood. The potato-pounding beetle was an important kitchen tool where animals were fed boiled potatoes. In some kitchens there was a hollow in the flag floor into which the freshly-boiled cauldron of spuds was placed direct from the crane. The hole held it secure whilst the contents were being pounded by the long-handled beetle. A mell was a homemade mallet used for pounding whins for the horses, and a similar kind of mallet was used for tenderising meat.

Wood was also used for making tray-type carriers, and for the frames of riddles and sieves. A piece of fine mesh and some small nails were all that was required to complete a homemade sieve.

Coiled food-baskets were widely used in the Aran Islands for transporting perishables or for holding food in the home. They had handles and resembled modern buckets. Calf-muzzles or calf-baskets were also woven, usually from rushes, and placed on the calf's head with the mouth covered.

Both pliable materials and wood were used by parents and children to make toys. A child adept at simple weaving could make a little basket for carrying nuts or fruit gathered in autumn. Children often made themselves 'pinkeen' nets for fishing in the local stream, or butterfly cages. And it wasn't unusual in my grandmother's day for a young girl to weave herself a straw or rush hat and decorate it with a daisy-chain or garland of wild roses. The results of her efforts might

---

Figure 46 A: two-storey hen's nesting-box; B: single nesting-basket; C: woven bucket; D: hanging nest-basket; E: netmaking – (a) net, (b) netting-needle; F: potato-basket for table; G: boater hat; H: turf-basket; I: net basket; J: egg-basket; K: woven wicker armchair for parlour.

Fig 46

not have been professional, but at least she derived infinite pleasure from making it herself.

Certain calendar events necessitated the making of ceremonial 'toys' and associated dress. My father can remember receiving a few sticks of 'Peggy's leg', the ubiquitous lucky bag, an orange, a whistle or bugle, and some mechanical toy or other in his stocking, hung at the end of the bed on Christmas Eve. But prior to that parents probably fashioned toys from wood or rushes and gave them to the children at Christmastime. I'm sure many a mother was delighted to dress her children up on St Stephen's Day and send them out to 'follow the wran'. The children invariably disguised themselves much as they do today, but the emphasis was on fun rather than on making money. They went to the trouble of seeking out a wren, of sacrificing it and suspending it from a bush; then they carried it from house to house chanting the words of the song:

> The wren, the wren,
> The king of all birds,
> St Stephen's Day was caught in the furze;
> Up with the kettle, and down with the pan,
> Give me a penny to bury the wran.

Everybody contributed towards the burial. The money didn't, however, find its way inevitably into the children's pockets, but was handed over at the end of the day to provide the drink and food for the evening's festivities. In some parts of the country straw-boys arrived at the local centre of the night's activity, though they generally appeared only at weddings in many areas. They were known as straw-boys because of their outfit which was made entirely from straw. In the Dingle area a *sor sop* or 'Sir Wisp', was a personage in the wren-play and was traditionally clad in a straw suit, masked, and armed with a wooden sword or pig's bladder fastened to a rod. He represented an Englishman, and was defeated in a combat by an Irish 'knight', similarly clad, and known as *Seán Scot*. The spectacle they put on was probably a great source of entertainment for youngsters.

Hallowe'en masks were known in the old days as vizards, and were made and worn by children, as were crosses. The children made their own masks and crosses and used blood, grass and soot to add colour to plain paper or cloth. On St Patrick's Day special badges, also

---

Figure 47 A: spale basket and weave; B: cane seat; C: basketmakers at work; D: garden trug; E: rest chair; F: wicker armchair; G: invalid's chair; H: *súgán* armchair.

A

B

C

D

E

F

G

H

Fig 47

shaped as crosses, were made, and again home-dyeing was used. Earlier in the year, on the feast of St Brigid, St Brigid's crosses were woven from rushes and worn by girls, along with special belts. And, of course, all young teenage girls knew how to make the four-legged crosses described in Chapter 5. The *brídeog* was an effigy of the saint, fashioned from old pieces of material and stuffed with straw or hay. A bonnet gave an appearance of reality to the head. The *brídeog* was mounted on a stick and carried by the leader, usually a young girl, in the St Brigid's day procession from house to house.

Games in rural Ireland consisted mainly of hurling, sling-shooting, football when a pig's bladder was available after a killing (see Chapter 12), and in my part of the country skittles was very popular. The Irish country folk were adept at amusing themselves, and *cluiche caointe* was the name used to describe the games people played at funeral wakes. These were often played in the form of pranks with the least intelligent members of the group the butt of the jokes!

Figure 48   A-D: St Brigid's crosses; E-G: corn knots; H: baby's rattle; I: potato-box; J: riddle; K: mussel-trap; L: horn spoon; M: mussel-trap; N: bacon-rolling tool, used to make joints for easy cooking; O: wire toasting-fork; P: lobster-pot.

Fig 48

Chapter 11

The Farmyard

The farmyard was the nucleus of the farm, the place where the major farm operations were discussed in great detail before commencing in the fields, the place where much of the winter work was done, and, perhaps most importantly, it was the link between farmhouse and land.

The farmyard as such was non-existent on some remote mountain farms. The normal farmyard activities were carried out on any piece of convenient ground in the vicinity of the dwelling-house or scattered outhouses, with the emphasis on shelter which was often a scarce commodity on east- or sea-facing slopes. Where there was more definition, such as having the sheds on one side of what was thought of as the farmyard, and the dwelling-house on the other, the farmyard space was invariably known as the *sráid* or street, while any narrow passageway leading off it was known as the *sráidín,* or little street. In my own locality, where the farmyard has always been known as the farmyard, the children of today are highly amused when they hear a new family in the district referring to their yard as a 'street'.

In the midlands and surrounding districts, the farmyard was essentially a courtyard, often with a hand-pump mounted on a stone platform above a trough in the very centre or close to the front door of the house. Sheds flanked the square or rectangular yard on two sides, with access to the haggard almost opposite the road-gate. In more recent times this pattern continued to prevail, but with the house backing onto the yard instead of opening onto it. A separate front yard filled with traditional sweet-scented cottage flowers, pots of colourful geraniums, and shrubs, had to be landscaped into the arrangement. A second gateway too was necessary, but only strangers ever used it; neighbours and friends continued to use the yard door, now known as the back door.

CHARACTER OF THE FARMYARD

The farmyard was generally bright and airy in summertime – despite the dunghill where the hens were continually scratching in search of grubs – but in winter it was often drab and quite damp if not properly maintained by the farmer. I can remember my grandparents' yard as a perfect square where docks and nettles flourished in summertime if given half a chance, and where one took one's life in one's hands after dark on a winter's evening if one tried to cross it when rain had fallen that day. Well-worn paths radiated from the front door through the forest of clipped weeds – one to the barn, one along the front of the building to the steps which led to the kitchen garden at the back, one to the milking shed, and a wide one to the gate. Because they had a clay surface these paths were treacherous after rain, until my father shovelled gravel onto them in later years.

The farmer had very little light in the yard as he went about his evening chores in the wintertime. A wide shaft of pale light was emitted through the doorway of the house, and a flickering beam from his storm-lamp lighted his way to some degree, but during icy or very wet conditions he was slipping and sliding all over the place, which couldn't have been much fun if he was carrying a pail of milk. Perhaps that was why most Irish farmers wore hobnailed boots, which, for all their weight and awkwardness, provided a good grip.

The farmyard was a good place for wildlife. A host of wild flowers flourished in abundance, their blooms adding a welcome touch of colour throughout the summer. Sycamore or beech trees provided shade in summer – sometimes too much shade – and shelter in wintertime. A 'fairy bush' often flourished close to the front door of the house, a harbinger of good luck. The fairy bush was, of course, the whitethorn or maybush and in early summer provided the family with a permanent maybush to decorate. Gorse, too, was considered lucky, and was generally grown close to the house because of its value as a clothes dryer.

The usual farmyard weeds were groundsel, dandelion (the leaves of which were fed to young turkeys), comfrey, docks, pineappleweed and burdock. Comfrey roots were ground down and taken internally to cure hiatus hernia, while the leaves of coltsfoot were dried and used as tobacco. Elder bushes were rarely found far from habitation in the old days, especially in the midlands, where it was generally accepted that the rather heavy smell of the elder kept butterflies at bay in early summer when they sought out cabbages on which to lay their eggs. The elder was also highly regarded as a medicinal plant; even the clay around the roots was said to cure toothache! The fermented berries made a palatable wine and cured cough spasms which accompanied summer colds.

Where a farmer lived alone and didn't have much time or interest in the maintenance of his yard, it was often a sorry sight indeed; overgrown with weeds and sometimes nettlebeds, it might have been fronted by a tumbledown stone wall with an old brass bed-end for a gate. Lichen-infested boulders often stood by the front door of the house – unsightly perhaps, but useful as makeshift seats in summertime. This arrangement was more common in western areas where the boulders were frequently strewn with damp fishing nets.

Midland and eastern farmyards almost always appeared more prosperous than those further west or south. A flock of mixed poultry in the yard helped enormously to give a good impression, and another impressive status symbol was a pump within sight of the road. The greater the size of the dunghill in early spring before the top-dressing got underway the better too, because the dunghill represented the farmer's wealth more obviously than anything else.

FARMYARD WORK

One of the most important farmyard chores was the sawing and chopping of firewood. The log (*cearchall* if it had been brought down by lightning or found in the bog, and *bloc* if it had been sawn from a tree on the land) was placed horizontally across a homemade sawing-trestle (see Figure 49). A saw was then used to slice the log into portions, which were then axed into smaller blocks. These were collected by the housewife or by the children and taken indoors to the fireside basket. At Christmas it was traditional for the father and children to bring home a *bloc na Nollag,* or Yule-log. This was either pulled by hand, using a chain or rope for extra leverage, or by donkey, and it had to be burned whole at the back of the fire.

In timber areas tree-felling was a specialised craft. Ideally it was an autumn job, carried out when the sap was down. Large logs of timber were either taken home in a horse-drawn sledge, or drawn by chain to the nearest sawing-pit – in those days most woods had sawing-pits located in clearings. The log was drawn over the centre of the pit opening (see Figure 49), and one man lowered himself into the depths of the narrow trench. The second man stood atop the log and together the two men sawed the big log lengthways, using a specially adapted saw, known as a pit-saw.

Other saws used for slicing different ways were the cross-cut saw, used by two men with a trestle, and the frame-saw, also known as the 'betteye' or 'dancing betty' and used as a simple hand-saw. Because

Figure 49 A: pit-saw; B: working a pit-saw of an earlier type; C: frame-saw; D: early auger; E: man using slaving-horse to help with planing; F: early hardwood drill; G: brace and two bits; H: very early (medieval and before) hole-boring instrument of most basic design; I: 'Jesus saw'; J: 'dancing betty', or frame-saw; K: using the two-man saw on homemade sawing trestle.

Fig 49

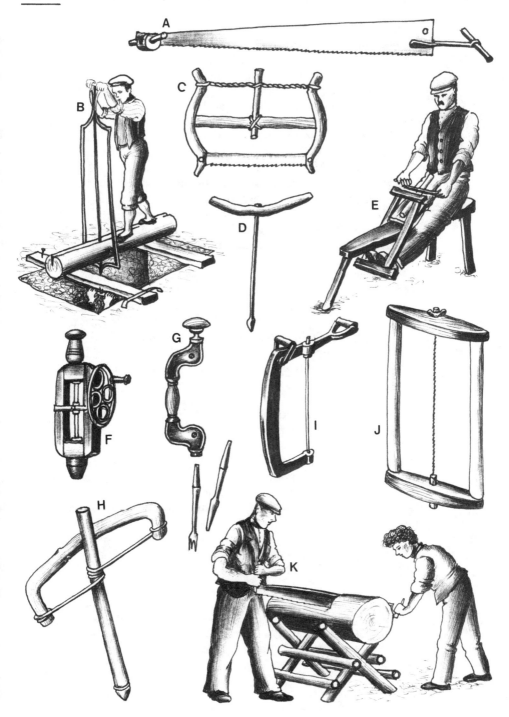

of all the nodding it did when used it was sometimes called a 'Jesus saw'.

One of the most important annual events centred around the farmyard was the threshing in wintertime, when the yard was alive with noise and excitement. Few threshing mills could get beyond the farmyard to the haggard, so, following a laboured entrance through the often very narrow gateway, it was parked in front of the house. The corn was carted from the haggard and threshed one load at a time. Small farmers who owned a small hand-thresher between ten or twelve of them also did their threshing in the yard on a fine day.

Other yard jobs included the slicing and pulping of vegetables for food for the animals. The poor farmer generally used an old scythe-blade with a wooden handle added, but the wealthier farmers had special machines for doing much of the work.

Wheelbarrows, gurry-butts and hand barrows were used for trans-porting tools, animal food and so on around the yard and its immediate environs. The *súgán* or burden rope (see Chapter 10) was used for transporting small lots of fodder to the fields in wintertime; the horse and cart or slide-car would have been used otherwise.

Oil-cake was one of the first imported cattle foods. When freshly bought it was very hard and came in large portions which had to be broken up. The farmer who could afford to feed cattle-cake to his cows could also probably afford the machine invented to break it up. Most of these machines had twin rollers like those of a laundry mangle, but with closely spaced spikes or ridges to break up the cake. In a typical machine the cake was dropped by hand into the hopper so that it fell down between the spiked rollers. The handwheel was geared down to increase strength. Small solid pieces were then fed as 'nuts' to cattle, while the powdery waste was added to the dung and spread out on the land.

Sieves were also used for preparing food for the animals, especially for young animals. Various beetles and mallets were used for breaking whins for the horses, and chaff-cutters for breaking down straw and chaff which was fed to cattle kept indoors during the wintertime. Sophisticated mechanical chaff-cutters like that shown in Figure 50 could be afforded only by wealthy farmers; and because of their dangerous toothed roller they were operated by the farmer himself and never by the children.

Figure 50 A: knife-sharpener; B: homemade turnip-slicer; C: turnip-knife with pick up hook at end; D: turnip-slicer; E: knife-grindstone; F: early root-slicer; G: steelyard; H: root-washer (follow arrows); I: chaff-grinder; J: root-washer, which doubled as potato grader; K-M: barley-hummelers; N: sack-hook.

Fig 50

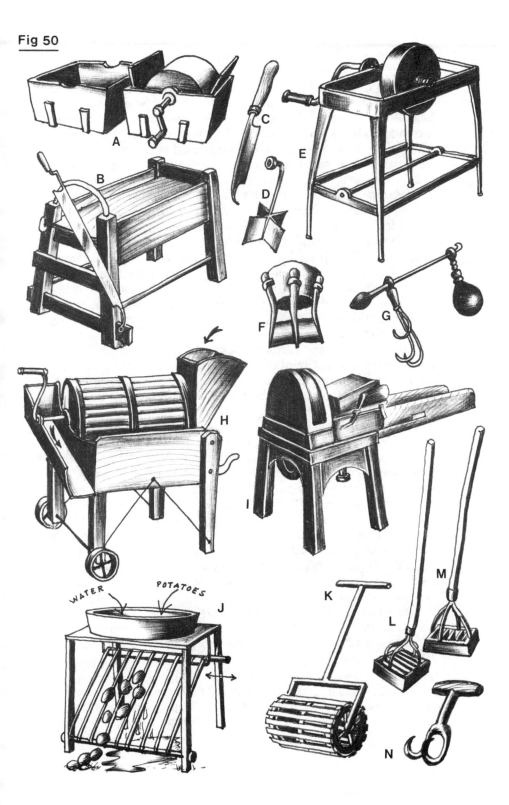

Some farmers had a small workshop. It served as a quiet retreat on a winter's day when attention was not demanded elsewhere on the farm. A sturdy bench, often the farmer's own creation, provided space on which to make handles for tools or little wooden vessels and holders for the home. A wooden tool-box was essential for holding the various chisels and so on, and this, too, was usually homemade. Most of the tools were much like those used today, except that in some cases handles and so on were very decorative. The somewhat primitive-looking auger dates back to medieval times. Some wooden-handled braces can be traced back to the 1700s. Tools with sharp blades were usually wrapped in straw to save the sharpness and the proud farmer polished the handles of his tools regularly.

Sometimes the local blacksmith was requested to call to a farmhouse with his portable forge. The smith was an important man in the locality, a veritable pillar of society. Generally, the local farmers brought their horses to the smith for shoeing, or took him their metal tools which needed repairs. However, in some areas a particular smith might have been known to be a travelling farrier who took his business to the farmers rather than have them take theirs to him. He travelled by horse and cart and took with him a portable forge, a hand-bellows, a small but heavy anvil and a wooden box filled with the tools he normally required. When he arrived in the yard he was always greeted effusively by the family, especially by the boys who thought the farrier was a hero, a sort of rural 'superman' of the day. They watched with a mixture of awe and excitement as he set up his forge. The container was filled with fuel supplied by the farmer – hard clods of peat, charcoal or coal – and set alight. A long-handled tongs was then used to hold strips of metal in the depths of the glowing red embers, which were encouraged into more glorious life from time to time with the help of the bellows, invariably worked by one or other of the children watching with giggling enthusiasm. When the metal was hot and red it was held on the anvil, again with the aid of tongs, and hammered into the desired shape while pliable. Once the shape had been acquired it was thrust into a tub or barrel of cold water where it spat and hissed until it had cooled down. It was then almost ready for use.

The smith wasn't just the local metal-worker, he was also the dentist in the old days. When a person was writhing with toothache the answer was to visit the blacksmith's forge and have the tooth out.

Figure 51 A: water diviner at work; B: yard-pump (metal); C: yard-pump (metal with wooden frame); D-E: hooks used for locating lost buckets in well; F: wooden pail; G: metal well-bucket; H: pump in winter 'coat' of straw; I: collecting water from river; J: water-ladle.

Fig 51

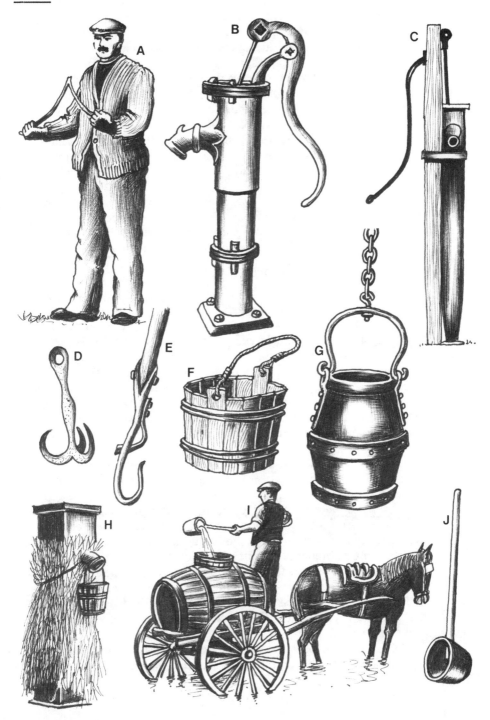

This was achieved by tying a piece of strong string to the tooth and also the anvil. The smith then offered a red-hot piece of metal to the sufferer who jerked away in horror and pulled his own tooth! The water which was used for quenching hot iron was a known cure for warts, boils and ugly eruptions, provided the skin wasn't open. And in some areas it was believed that if the same water were applied to a squinty eye three mornings in succession without the smith's knowledge, it would cure the squint.

The smith also treated horses. Saddle-sores and bruises were treated with washes, using the water from the trough, and he could flush out a horse's nose with a syringe he made himself from a pig's bladder. He also used fleams and other instruments described in Chapter 12.

The smith was a revered member of the community and on feastdays his clients invariably sent him a plucked bird, a sack of potatoes or some such gift. Even poorer farmers who couldn't afford to give him money for his service often paid him with food.

ODD JOBS ON THE LAND

Here I've grouped a selection of chores which were done only when the important jobs described in earlier chapters were dispensed with. One of these chores was weeding in the garden or farmyard. Such troublesome plants as chickweed, charlock, dock and thistle were nuisances, choking up vegetable crops and forming unsightly little crops of their own in the yard. Root-lifters were special tools designed for removing whole plants which were too tough for pulling by hand from the ground. A swallow-tailed root-lifter was used to lift out awkward tap-roots, but for less troublesome plants the metal or wooden weeding-tongs sufficed. Sometimes a farmer merely dug out weeds.

Drainage was another important chore, usually reserved for wintertime. Gripe-making, or 'ditching' as it was known in the northern counties, was one of the best ways of draining land. Deep wide trenches were excavated by hand or plough along the field boundaries. In wintertime excess water drained into the trenches from the land, but in summer both land and trenches were dry. Bushes and tree branches fell out in a canopy over the dry trenches, making excellent shelters for cows who sought their shade as a refuge from both sun and ever-present flies. The alternative to trench-draining was pipe-drainage. Heavy pipes were laid down in the trenches and covered over. They took the water away in summer as well as in winter.

The production of water for domestic use usually involved the sinking of a well. This required the services of a water diviner. He arrived armed with a bundle of hazel (forked sticks) and chose one from the bundle. Then, holding it lightly in both hands – palms facing upwards and thumbs outwards – he kept the point of the fork forwards and slowly walked over the ground. Once the fork twitched upwards of its own volition he had stepped onto ground directly above a water channel. A mark was etched on the ground with his heel and he continued on, finding other channels and following them until he found a spot where they met or crossed. If he was a good water diviner he could estimate to the nearest inch from the pressure on his divining rod just how deep the water flowed. Some diviners actually shook like a leaf with intense reaction when they located water, and in most cases sweat broke out on the forehead and the breathing became laboured, a source of great awe to the youngsters.

The yard-pump was an important asset on any farm. It saved the housewife trips to the nearest well, and provided the farmer with water when he was preparing animal food and when he was cleaning out the stables and sheds. In the case of a hand-pump, it was usually mounted on a stone platform with a stone or wooden trough underneath to catch the water; in the case of a draw-well, a rope with a crook at the end from which a pail was suspended was lowered into the dark depths of a chasm until water was reached. A handle was turned to lower and raise the pail, and usually a thatched roof protected the water below. A stone wall, as high as could be built, surrounded the opening so that children didn't fall in.

The creation of water-meadows in some low-lying areas was known in localities where the river flowed at almost the same level as surrounding land. The chosen flat fields were drowned and then allowed to become lodged. When other fields were scorched by frost during the winter months, the water meadows maintained a higher temperature beneath the carpet of water and when drained in spring-time developed into early grazing or meadows.

FENCING AND HEDGING

Finally in this chapter we look at fencing and hedging. These were winter chores. Nowadays, fencing refers almost exclusively to the erection of barbed wire fences which criss-cross the fields of Ireland, but in the old days the job of fencing was the actual repair work done to hedges – trimming of overgrown bushes with a billhook, also known as a slasher, and the filling in of gaps. This was more or less a perennial chore, but hedging, which was the creation of a new strip of hedge, might only be done twice or three times in a farmer's lifetime. The hedged-ditch, described in Chapter 7, was built and trees were planted intermittently along its length, usually ash or sycamore. Once the briary hedging began to flourish the barrier became a haven for wildlife: the earthen bank might be riddled with badger sett entrances, birds sang happily and built their nests in the bushes, and wild flowers, which attracted a myriad of insects throughout the summer, formed a colourful herbaceous border along the base of the hedge.

When barbed wire and post fencing was introduced it represented a major breakthrough in the agricultural world because it meant that a farmer could build a barrier in a very short time and take it down if he no longer needed it. However, these sterile barriers didn't attract any wildlife whatsoever, nor did they provide any shelter for animals, and although farmers of my father's generation sing their praises, the older folk regard them with certain disapproval.

When barbed wire was introduced, new tools were also introduced to assist the fencer. For instance, a post-hole spade was used to make the holes for the uprights. Wire-drawers or stretchers were used to draw the wire taut between posts. One tool was worked with a screw-thread, another operated by a long lever and ratchet mechanism. Early barbed wire was much different from the thorny twisted strands we know today. Jagged pieces of metal simply sat at intervals on smooth wire, and were shaped like stars, triangles, etc. And until such time as the shapes became loose and wandered along the wire, they were just as effective as modern barbs.

Figure 52 A-B: pattens used to raise feet above soft mud or bogland; C: digging 'foot'; D: boot fitted with digging 'foot'; E: 'legging'; F-H: types of slasher; I-I(a): wire-puller; J: barbs; K-L: mud-spades; M: trench-spade; N: trench-shovel; O: drain-scoop; P: drain-spade; Q: early drainage-pipe.

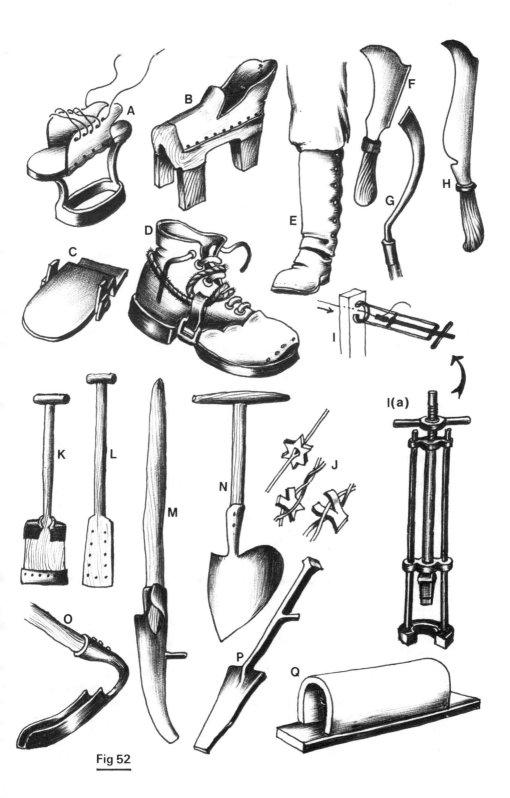

Fig 52

Chapter 12

The Animals

The animals were an important part of the Irish farm of old not just because they were bred as a source of income, but also because some of them were beasts of burden known by name to the family and treated almost as pets – the donkey in particular.

The old breeds are rarely seen today, especially in the case of poultry, pigs and cattle. Only horses and donkeys have remained the same, and this is probably due to the fact that their usefulness became obsolete with the advent of steam and later the combustion engine, and so no scientific animal breeders interfered with them 'in the name of progress'.

There have always been three principal breeds of horse – the Irish Draught, the Shire from England, and the Clydesdale from Scotland. The Irish Draught was big and powerful, with a thickset, short-legged build, and unlike other carthorse breeds it had no 'beard' on its legs. The Shire was a strong animal too, but because of its easy-going nature was more suited to the slow farmer who wasn't in any particular hurry to get the work done. The Shire tended to amble along at snail's pace, but not through laziness. He was very reliable and never tried to shirk his duty, however burdensome. Nowadays we are familiar with bay or brown Shires, but during the 1800s they were invariably piebald or even skewbald. The Clydesdale was much faster, but much more temperamental too, given to nervous bouts which often resulted in fits of bolting and stubbornness. However, it was virtually free of leg troubles, a bonus to any farmer.

Individual horses were well known to the local blacksmith, and when fitting a new shoe outfit he often corrected faults in gait and the consequences of previous injury or disease. Sturdy males, or stallions, were often walked miles across the countryside to service mares in heat, and in the case of a Shire, the stallion often weighed as much as a ton! Stallions used for servicing mares had to be in good condition and were often examined by the local blacksmith prior to the mating season.

The donkey was, in effect, the poor man's horse, a loyal beast of burden, content with a field of thistles and the odd pail of oats. Donkeys ranged in appearance from the shaggy little 'asaleen' (from *asal*, 'a donkey') to the sleek mule-like ass with a mind of its own! I can remember seeing a cousin of mine mount my father's donkey with confident enthusiasm, only to be bucked off right over the animal's head almost before the ride had begun.

Goats too had their moments, especially during the mating season when bucks came 'from the short grass' to mate with nannies. Usually the nannies were tethered in the garden or yard, but even with gates closed this presented no problems to the buck, or billy-goat as he was sometimes known. Bucks were renowned for their ability to leap great heights, right over a hedge if need be. Not alone that – they brought with them a stink which hung in the air for days after they'd gone!

Generally, the goats came originally from the Alpine countries, Switzerland in particular. But a long-eared bleater with a distinctive Roman nose, known as the Nubian goat, came from central Africa. The Anglo-Nubian gave an excellent supply of rich milk. Other good milkers were the horned (both sexes) black and white Schwartzal, the white Saanens and Toggenburgs. Some families liked to have a goat in addition to the cows for it was generally accepted that goat's milk was better than cow's milk for human consumption. Also, goats didn't get either tuberculosis or brucellosis. However, goats did tend to disrupt progress in the garden by nibbling voraciously at every-thing in sight if they got half a chance!

The sheep farmer was restricted by his land in his choice of animals. Most of the native breeds were suited to rough upland ground, as were the imported Scottish Blackface and Cheviot. Other breeds with dense coats like the Oxford Downs, Suffolks and Lincolns – all imported breeds – did well on low ground. However, if they shared good land with cattle, they invariably suffered from foot rot and other diseases; low, bad land was necessary for their healthy survival.

The male sheep was the ram or tup, and the female was the ewe (pronounced yeo). A castrated ram was known as a wether or widar, and a yearling which didn't yet have its coat removed was known as a hogget. Sheep were kept mainly for their wool, which was sold either to the local spinner or at the mart. It earned the farmer little more than a pittance, just about keeping bellies full in poorer areas.

Cattle breeds of old included the diminutive Dexter and Kerry (not from county Kerry). Squat, short-legged animals, they were good milkers, could fatten rapidly when required, and were very adaptable to the harsh conditions of mountain farming. But they've been supplanted in almost all areas by Friesians and others.

The larger breeds of the old days were the Red-Polls and Black-Polls (having no horns), bred as dual-purpose animals for their milk and meat, and Dairy Shorthorns which were hardy and thrifty and good milkers. Beef Shorthorns were bred as cattle, rarely as cows, and sold for good money at the fair.

Pigs were bred in large numbers by wealthy farmers; poorer farmers generally only kept a few for home consumption. Spotted and barred varieties, like the Gloucester Old Spot and the Saddleback, were popular with small-holders and the Large White from Yorkshire was widely bred for its fleshy pork.

Poultry, which included hens, ducks, turkeys and geese, were kept by every housewife in the old days. They were her responsibility and she kept the money she received for both poultry and eggs. The breeds of old were very different from those of today – hybrids were unknown; all hens were broody, and unlike their modern counterparts were good layers for much longer than two or three years! When my grandmother was setting up home she kept Rhode Island Reds which were a new breed; nowadays they are classed as an old breed. She also kept Light Sussex and Wyandotte, handsome broody birds and surprisingly good layers when properly fed. And when their laying life was over they were either allowed to grow old gracefully in the farmyard with the younger hens, or they were killed for the pot. Tenderness was achieved by boiling the birds prior to roasting.

Hens are intelligent and interesting birds. Once a hen established a good laying spot, whether it was a sheltered part of the hedge, the cow's manger or the nest provided in the hen-house, she invariably stuck with it throughout the laying season. She also laid at the same time each day. However, since the hen wasn't a modest creature and liked to boast about her daily deposit, my grandmother could detect the location of the laying spot by listening for the inevitable loud cackle of triumph. When a hen was clucking she was ready for hatching, but this didn't always suit my grandmother – she often put the hen under an upturned pot until the broodiness went off her, otherwise the hen would be a hatching hen and would sit on eggs until the birds hatched out.

Figure 53 A: shoeing a horse in the yard; B: travelling smith's forge, consisting of portable forge (a), small anvil (b) and toolbox (c); C: veterinary tooth-extractor; D: cramps; E: Gloucester Old Spot pig; F: bull-pole; G: Cochin chicken; H: Frizzle chicken; I: Dexter cow; J: anti-suckling device; K: Anglo-Nubian goat; L: horn-straightener; M: pincers and bull's nose-ring.

Fig 53

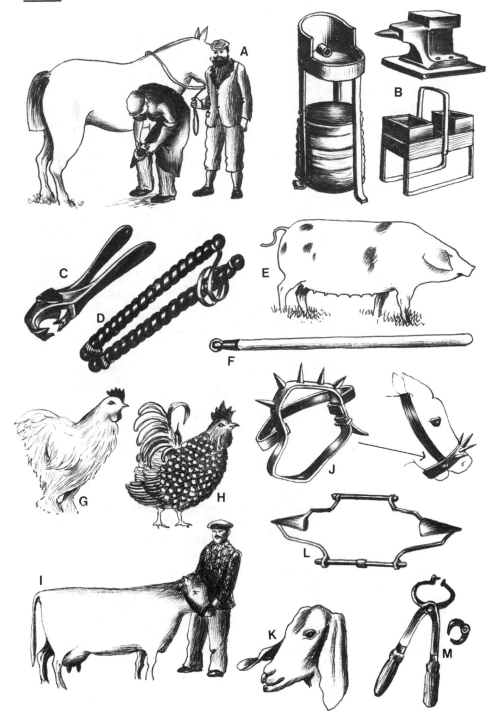

Copulating with the farmyard cockerel was nothing if not brazenly spectacular, visible for all to see. The cock, oftentimes as wicked and cantankerous as the gander or turkey-cock, approached his chosen hen with a boldly suggestive strut and raced forward to confront any opposition from other cocks when there were more than one. At daybreak he took up his customary position on the dunghill and crowed loudly, waking up the whole locality, and throughout the day he defended his 'harem'.

Cock-fighting was a cruel sport of the old days. A known venue was invaded by hordes of betting spectators after Mass on certain Sundays and specially groomed fighting cocks were put in a pit and encouraged to fight each other to the death. Thankfully, the sport has been illegal since 1849. It is said that to improve the fighting ability of a cock an unscrupulous cock-owner placed fresh eggs in the nest of the hawk so that any cocks which hatched out developed the characteristics of their adoptive parents. The best-known game breeds were the Duckwing, a pert little fellow renowned for his bravery, and the Blackcaps and Redcaps. Spangles were a popular fighting breed too, and all were 'dubbed' – they had their tail feathers and combs trimmed with a special scissors before stepping into the pit. Steel and silver spiked spurs were fitted to the legs to ensure a nasty ending to a bloodthirsty event.

Exotic breeds of hen were bred on some farms for their egg production, despite their impractical appearance. The feathery Cochin with the 'baggy trouser' legs and the fancy Brahmas from Asia were two popular breeds, and Frizzles of course, with their curled up plumage, were terrific layers. Other more conventional-looking hens included the Cuckoo Maran, the North Holland Blue, the Favorelle, the Ancona and Andalusian from Spain, and the various Leghorns. Very few of any of the above can be found on farms today; they've been largely replaced by the Golden Comet and similar hybrids.

In the old days my grandmother had what was known as a turkey-station, to which other women took their female turkeys to be serviced by my grandmother's fearsome turkey-cock. In those days turkeys, although known as Bronzes, were black in colour. The geese, on the other hand, were pure white, and the gander was just as fierce as the turkey-cock, defending his territory with a threatening hiss and following anyone who bothered him. Embden geese have been bred

Figure 54 A: mouth-gag; B: bleeding-fleam; C: feeding-trough; D: sheep, wearing yoke; E: shearing-clips; F: shearing with an early shearing-machine; G: dipping-crook; H: branding; I: sheep's anti-scratching collar; J: shepherd's crook; K: pair of dipping-crooks; L: pair of collar bells.

Fig 54

in Ireland since the early 1800s, but prior to that Pilgrim geese were bred, and were noted for their grey geese and white ganders. A small breed, the Roman goose, was introduced during the 1900s. Aylesbury ducks were popular on farms which didn't rely too much on duck-eggs but rather on duck meat, whereas Indian Runners, attractive upright ducks, were excellent egg-producers.

LOOKING AFTER THE ANIMALS

The animals required their share of attention, and most of this was administered by the farmer or a visiting 'quack' animal doctor. Sometimes the local smith helped, but until recent times there were no veterinary surgeons.

Restraining was the biggest problem in the days of no hypodermics, especially in the case of a heavy farmhorse or bull. Restraining devices were invented to combat the problem – devices such as the horse-twitch, consisting of a loop of string attached to a pole and used to grip the horse's lip or tongue, and the 'cramps' which consisted of two twisted bars of wood used in much the same way. For bulls, a bull-pole was often attached to the copper ring permanently fitted in the animal's nostril. If the bull made a move, a twist of the bull-pole was enough to send him into paroxysms of pain.

The local 'quack' performed surgery, and for this a bull, for instance had to be temporarily blindfolded with a leather bull-blind. A horse which kicked a lot had its legs tied with hobbles during surgery and a canvas bag was placed over its head. A nose-clamp was sufficient restraint for cows or young cattle, although horned animals had to have a rope tied tightly around the horns if they were not to injure the farmer. Pigs, with their high-pitched screeching, had little one could grasp if one discounted the ears, so they invariably presented a problem. A noose tied around the jaw was fairly successful but it generally took more than two men to hold the animal down.

Sheep were normally light enough to be handled successfully by one man. A sheep's yoke was a home-made device which kept the sheep from wandering from field to field through narrow gaps, but when placed permanently in a shed or pen it held the animal still

---

Figure 55   A: pig-gib; B: bacon-hook; C: piercing-stick; D: shaving-knife; E: shaving-knife; F: drenching-horn; G: branding-iron; H: docking-iron; I: branding-iron; J: docking-iron with sharp blade; K: shearing-machine (1930s); L: lambing-forceps; M: woven beeskep in specially built hut; N: woven beeskep in hole in the wall; O: fumigator; P-Q: woven beeskeps; R: wooden beeskep.

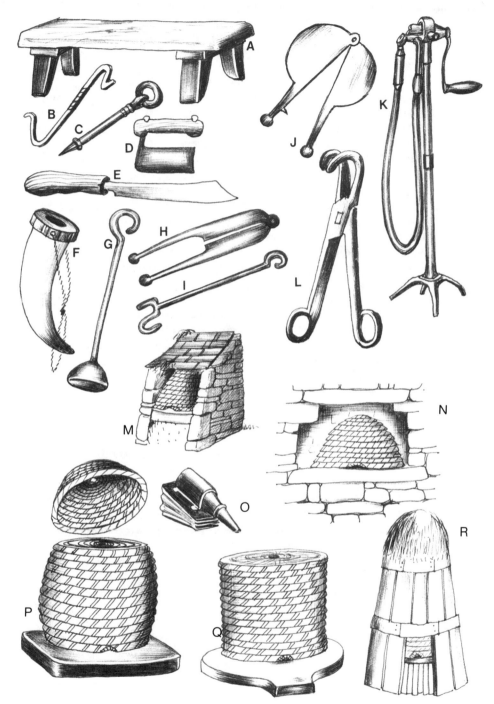

Fig 55

during treatment. A special sheep's collar kept a sheep from nibbling at wounds on its flank by preventing the head from turning.

All medicines were administered orally, using a balling-gun or flexible probang, or if they were liquid they were given as a drench using an old cow's horn. A medicine pellet was known as a bolus. It might have been made from a powder ground down in a pestle and mortar by the farmer himself, and to make it go through more easily to the animal's throat a metal mouth-gag made by the smith kept the mouth open to give the farmer more leverage. Dough containing finely chopped pieces of garlic, a favourite cure-all of old, was rolled into neat balls and flicked into the animal's mouth.

Horse 'whisperers' were weird country folk who practised a form of magic bordering on the black arts and exhibited strange powers over horses. And, of course, the poor old fairies were blamed for every ailment of both man and beast. Oddly enough, when a shed was built on a 'fairies' pass' animals seemed to get sick for no apparent reason whenever they were put into that particular shed, and only the 'quack' could break the spell.

Fleams or bleeding instruments were used to release blood from an ailing animal, a custom born of the notion that bleeding helped to relieve symptoms. A set of fleams consisting of different-sized blades for different-sized animals resembled a pocket knife set and was carried around in the pocket in the same way. The blood was taken from the animal's jugular vein and a horsehair was wound into a figure of eight and placed against the open wound with the help of a pin as an aid to fast healing. Horsehair was used too to remove the tiny worms which caused the pick, a sort of intense wheezing, in chickens. The single horsehair was looped at one end, then plaited and thrust down the chicken's throat, and when it was brought back up a tiny worn wriggled in the loop. The worm had usually been picked up in the dungheap.

Powerful, aggressive bulls were fitted with copper nose rings to help with restraint. A nose-punch, a pincer-like tool, worked like a paper punch to remove a small ring of cartilage from between the nostrils. The ring was then fitted and secured with a tiny screw.

Dehorning is a relatively painless experience for cattle nowadays, but in olden times it was a cruel but often necessary chore, especially where groups of cattle were housed together or penned together in small paddocks or fields. The farmer or local 'quack' used a saw to remove the horns to the resounding bellows of the pained animals, and then the bleeding wounds were dressed with a solution of Jeyes Fluid. The cattle were kept indoors if possible until the risk of infection had passed. Another painful experience, this time for young male calves, was castration. It was important to do this in fine but not necessarily hot weather, preferably in June when flies were scarce. A sharp knife or hot iron was used to release the testes from the scrotum, and a set of special clamps was attached to the cord to induce insensibility to the organ. Young lambs were castrated with a forceps.

WORKING WITH ANIMALS

Various jobs involving animals took place during the year. In early summer, for instance, the sheep farmer was occupied for weeks with the shearing. The services of the *spailpíns* (nomadic workers) was always welcomed at this time, for shearing involved a lot of slow, laborious work, especially if a hand shears was used. The shears, also known as clips, was replaced on well-to-do farms by hand-operated shearing machines which helped to reduce the workload considerably for the farmer. A cratch was a sort of bench used when working with the shears; alternatively the shearer squatted on the ground and held the sheep against him, or stood over the animal, giving his back cause to complain later!

The killing of the 'barrow' (the fat pig), was an important event on any farm because it marked the beginning of a regular meat supply for months to follow. The local slaughterer (*búistéir*) a man experienced in the rustic art of pig-killing, was approached to do the job, though some farmers killed their own pigs. When the *búistéir* arrived the whole family gathered round to watch the killing. His first job was to plunge a knife into the pig's heart via the throat, using a special knife. The screeching during this performance was something awful, but the animal died instantly once the heart had been reached, usually to a round of applause from the onlookers. The animal was then draped across a pig-gib, a sort of bench, and had the fine hairs on its body scraped off. To make this a simple job the animal was immersed in hot water a number of times until the bristles were softened and easy to remove. If a few hairs were accidentally missed the bacon would be known as 'hairy bacon'!

The carcass was now suspended from a hook in one of the sheds so that it could drip naturally into a basin placed under its head. A potato placed in the mouth helped the dripping process. The carcass remained thus for a couple of days, and when my father was a boy he had an intense but irrational fear of the hanging pig in the shed and wouldn't go in alone to see it if his life depended on it!

When the *búistéir* returned he had to slit the carcass open and remove the bones. The head was chopped off and weighed, and my father maintains that for every pound weight of head there was a corresponding stone weight of body. Cold water was used to wash the carcass and a barrel was brought out to accommodate the pieces, which had to be properly salted if they were not to spoil during the 'seasoning' or curing period which followed. Every single crack on the meat had to be rubbed thoroughly with salt, then the pieces were placed one on top of the other neatly in the barrel. Then during the curing, regular checks were necessary to ensure that 'the pickle was rising'. In my own part of the midlands brown sugar was sometimes added to the salted meat to sweeten it. The barrel was covered over with extreme care, hermetically sealed to keep all air out.

No part of the pig went to waste, and I often heard my father remark that if they'd been able to capture the squeal they'd have made tin whistles out of it! The heart or pluck was kept for eating, as was the stomach which was known as chitlings. The feet, also known as trotters or crubeens (*crúibíní*), were boiled and eaten with cabbage. Homemade sausages and black-puddings were made, the latter from the blood, and encased in the intestines which were washed well and turned inside-out beforehand. The head was also eaten, traditionally with an apple in its mouth. The spine of a hog or the lean part of pork loin was known as the *griscín* and was suitable for broiling or roasting. And the bladder invariably ended up being kicked around the yard by the youngsters. A goose-quill was stuck into the neck of the bladder and after some fierce blowing, by each child in turn, it resembled a football – but it wasn't noted for its long life.

Salted meat took two weeks to cure. Then the flitches were removed and the *griscín* sliced off for cooking. A wealthy farmer took a selection of *griscíns* round to his poorer neighbours so that they could celebrate the killing of the pig. The rest of the flitches were hung up to keep.

Not all bacon was cured with salt. In some areas it was traditional to suspend the carcass from the chimney pole above a continuously burning fire of oak for about a week or so. Again, the flitches were hung up afterwards, preferably close to the hearth where they continued to benefit from the smoke.

Bee-keeping was an important occupation in the old days, for drinks such as mead and diluted honey were taken regularly to ward off colds, and honey was eaten with many plain foods before the introduction of sugar. A hive or two of bees might have been kept in the orchard or kitchen garden. The hive itself might have been built into a recess in a wall, or incorporated in a hut with stone constructed

Figure 56 A: rabbit-snare; B: bird-trap; C: large gin trap; D: bird-trap; E: 'humane' rodent-trap; F: rat-trap; G: early mouse-trap; H: box mouse-trap; I: rabbit and similar sized animals were trapped with this pole-trap; J: egg trap, sprung when weight of egg was removed; K: 'humane' man-trap; L: more lethal man-trap.

Fig 56

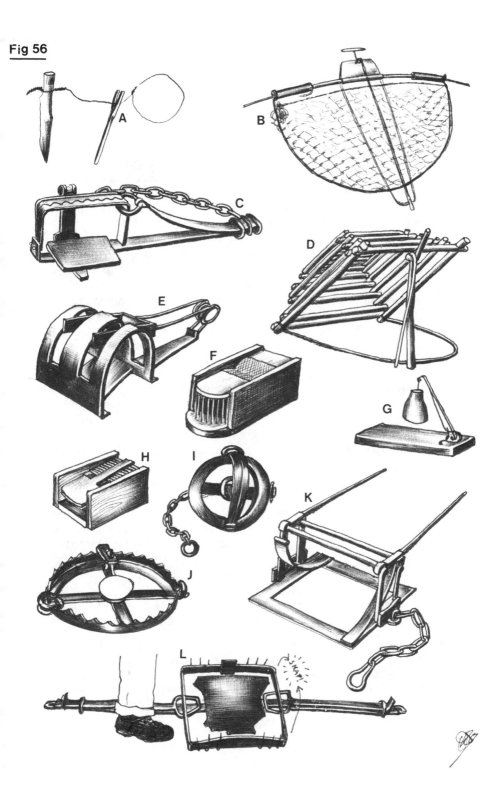

around it, or simply stood on a wooden platform. There were some wooden hives, but the straw-woven skep (*coirceog*) was by far the most common. Some of them were crudely constructed and resembled small cocks of hay from a distance. The neatly-made *ciséan* (to distinguish it from the above) was made by lipwork and had a lid which could be removed. It lasted a long time if properly handled. A small fumigator, used to stun the bees into silence for any major interruption, was sometimes used, but most bee-keepers will tell you that the bees know their master and won't harm him. In the old days it was traditional for a bee-keeper to inform the bees when a member of his family died, otherwise it was said they would fly off and set up home somewhere else!

Sometimes in a hard winter the bees might all be lost and one of the farmer's supplementary incomes went with them. However, it wasn't a substantial loss because the farmer only got a decent crop of honey once in every three years or so, and a bumper crop once in seven or more. Homemade honey, however scarce in the cupboard, was a valuable, inexpensive substitute for sugar, and was good for the health too. A single beehive meant a substantial saving for the housewife.

TRAPPING AND POACHING

Poaching was a serious business in some areas, and as with other illegal practices there were common-or-garden poachers who did it because of poverty at home, but also the totally unscrupulous characters who stopped at nothing to get a couple of fish to sell for a pittance. Many a bailiff and landlord turned a blind eye to the occasional poaching done by their poorer tenants, but very few tolerated the use of poisons or the catching of fish by the netload. For instance Irish spurge known as *báinnicín* was collected, placed in a sack and pounded so that the poisonous juices escaped. When hurled into the water all life for a hundred yards in either direction fell victim to the poison in a matter of minutes and the fish came floating to the surface, dead. Trout, perch and pike were taken, but minnows and other small fishes were left behind, innocent, unwanted victims of the poacher's blackguardism.

Sometimes a landlord took the precaution of setting a lethal mantrap to catch any poacher who might venture onto his land. Powerful

---

Figure 57 A: eel-spear; B: mud spear, Co. Westmeath; C: rock spear; D: salmon-spear, of type known in Co. Down area; E: spear-tooth; F: river-net; G: gaping river-net for salmon, Donegal; H: lethal eel spear-rake, fashioned from teeth of wool comb set into metal hold; I: woven eel-trap; J: coracle and paddle; K: wooden cot boat; L: river and sea rowing boat.

Fig 57

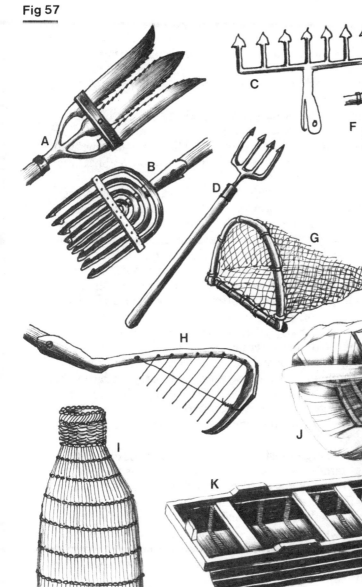

snapping jaws with needle teeth sank into the flesh of the leg, injuring the victim for life. Similar traps were used for trapping badgers, foxes and deer, and a homemade snare like that shown in Figure 56 was strategically constructed on a rabbit's run close to a warren to capture a rabbit for supper.

In 1714 the spearing of salmon was made illegal, but of course it continued after dark on some rivers. In fact it was practised openly in Galway city well into the last century. Tickling and 'gingling' with horsehair loops were common ways of baiting salmon, and nets were used to get them from the water.

Eels were caught illegally with longlines, but a more usual practice was to bait them with balls of worms, a practice called 'bobbing'. In parts of the north a vicious-looking implement known as an eel-rake was carried by the poacher at night and jabbed amongst the water-reeds where the eels fed. The implement, shown in Figure 57, was usually fashioned from an old flax or wool comb and was extremely dangerous. Pikes and spears were also used to catch fish. In the midlands a rock spear was used for spearing salmon and a less vicious mud spear for spearing eels.

Long ago a farmer rarely possessed a gun, so in order to capture animal meat for the dinner he either snared his quarry or hunted it, alone or with dogs. In my own area targets were aimed at with stones in practice sessions until a man became really adept at hitting his quarry in flight. Rabbits and hares were often caught in this manner. Foxes were not hunted for their meat, but were trapped or smoked in their dens as punishment for stealing poultry. Rarely did a farmer ever sell a fox skin.

This chapter illustrates just as clearly as the previous ones that the Irish farming family of old was a resilient, self-sufficient and adaptable group of people, who relied on their wits and intelligence to get by. The Famine undermined much of their slowly acquired confidence, but it didn't undermine it altogether. Once they picked themselves up again, they made significant progress over the years and are as far advanced in the world of modern agriculture as are most of their European counterparts today – much more advanced than some of them.

Yet, for all that I often wonder if we are not going backwards instead of forwards: no longer are the meadows filled with glorious wildlife, no longer is the haymaking and harvesting a social event, no longer is there any character to the Irish farm. The modern farmer is always in a hurry, has no time to chat with neighbours, yet, ironically, because of modern technology we have less to do than our ancestors. Perhaps the old ways were the best ways after all?

Acknowledgements

Most of the illustrations in this book were made from sketches done by the author in museums (see list below), but she wishes to acknowledge also some works used as a source for drawings and text:

Crafts of Ireland, Louise O'Brien, Gilbert Dalton, Dublin, 1979.
Irish Vernacular Architecture, Kevin Danaher, Mercier Press, Cork, 1975.
Irish Folk Ways, E. E. Evans, Routledge and Kegan Paul, London, 1957.
Life and Tradition in Rural Ireland, Timothy O'Neill, J. M. Dent and Sons, London, 1977.
Shire Albums, produced by Shire Publications, Buckinghamshire, England.
Shadows On Glass, Brian Mercer Walker, Appletree Press, Belfast, 1976.

Bunratty Folk Park, Co. Clare
Folk Museum, Muckross House, Killarney, Co. Kerry
Farm Museum, Johnstown Castle, Wexford
Folk Museum, Knock, Co. Mayo
Folk Museum, Glencolumbkille, Co. Donegal
Pighouse Museum, Co. Cavan, Ireland
Ulster Folk and Transport Museum, Cultra Manor, Holywood, Co. Down.

Welsh Folk Museum, St. Fagans, Cardiff, Wales
West Highland Folk Museum, Kingussie, Scotland
Beamish Open Air Museum, near Durham, England
Bicton Gardens Folk Museum, Devon, England
Weald and Downland Open Air Museum, Hampshire, England.

Other Books from The O'Brien Press

PERSONAL HEALTH RECORD
A passport-sized permanent record for all information about your family's health from birth onwards. Invaluable.

£3.99 hb

A THORN IN THE SIDE
Fr Pat Buckley

The story of his life and career, and thoughts on issues of contemporary life, from this radical priest.

£9.99 pb

UNIVERSITIES & COLLEGES IN THE UK
The Irish Student's Essential Guide
P.M. McGoldrick

The best guide for all students thinking of third-level study in the UK. Fully comprehensive.

£7.99 pb

THE OUTRAGEOUS GUIDE TO THE WORLD CUP
Paul Farrell & Graeme Keyes

An outrageously funny and irreverent guide to the World Cup – its history, the teams, the countries, the grandparent rule; Irish football from St Patrick to Jack Charlton. Lots of cartoons.

£4.99 pb

THE OFFICIAL GREEN ARMY JOKE BOOK
John Byrne

80 pages chockful of jokes and cartoons about football, the players, the journalists, the fans, the Boss. The essential pocket-size, take-anywhere accessory for fans aged nine to ninety.

£3.50 pb

LOTTERY
Michael Scott

Winning the Lottery catapults Christine Quinn into the world of the super-rich. Then dark shadows of her nightmare past appear, threatening to destroy her new-found happiness.

£4.99 pb

A VOICE FOR SOMALIA
President Mary Robinson

A first-hand account by the President of her historic visit to famine-stricken Somalia; her day-by-day diary, and hopes and suggestions for the future.

£6.95 pb

A BOOK OF IRISH QUOTATIONS
Edited by Sean McMahon

'A major insight into Ireland...' J.P. Donleavy, IRISH LITERARY REVIEW

£5.95 hb

THE STUNT
Shay Healy

Forget all that popstar do-goodery of U2 and Bob Geldof, *Poison Pig* just want to get rich quick and have a good time doing it. And with their slimy manager, 'Snake'O'Reilly, pulling the strings and organising the ultimate publicity stunt, their dreams of the big time look set to become real ...

£5.95 pb

SLIGO
Land of Yeats' Desire
John Cowell

An evocative account of the history, literature, folklore and landscapes, with eight guided tours of the city and county, from one who spent his childhood days in the Yeats country in the early years of this century. Illustrated.

£9.95 pb

TRADITIONAL IRISH RECIPES
George L. Thomson

Handwritten in beautiful calligraphy, a collection of favourite recipes from the Irish tradition.

£3.95 pb

SMOKEY HOLLOW
Bob Quinn

Worm's eye view of how children managed to survive parents in the dark ages before TV. Halfway between city and country, between domestic piety and street vulgarity, between Irish aspirations and British acculturation, the Toner children, Bob Quinn's fictionalised version of his own clan, explore all these alternatives to the full.

£5.95 pb

WEST CORK WALKS
Written & illustrated by Kevin Corcoran

Experience the rugged wildness of Ireland's most southerly region in the company of an expert naturalist. Walking in West Cork offers an incredible variety of choice - mountainous peaks, rolling heaths, forested valleys, pristine lakes, sandy beaches. 10 walks, spread across West Cork. Caters for casual strollers, family groups, ramblers, serious walkers. Beautifully illustrated with maps and line drawings.

£5.95 pb

KERRY WALKS
Written & illustrated by Kevin Corcoran

A superb walking guide to the wilderness and beauty of Kerry. Kevin Corcoran introduces Kerry's varied habitats and their wild inhabitants - heathland and bog, Ireland's highest mountains, coastal peninsulas, beaches, dunes, islands, forests, rivers, lakes. 20 walks, spread throughout the county. Maps, line drawings and colour photographs.

£7.95 pb

WEST OF IRELAND WALKS
Written & illustrated by Kevin Corcoran

Explore the counties of Clare, Galway and Mayo in the company of a wildlife expert. The walker will experience the West's marvellous wealth of wildlife: hills and cliffs, bog, mountain, woodland, sea fjord, lake shore, beaches. Superb illustrations by the author, who is a biologist, naturalist and conservationist. The walks vary from gentle to tough, but most are moderate. There is a detailed guide on distance, time, and level of difficulty. Maps and line drawings.

£5.95

ORDER FORM

Please send me the books as marked
I enclose cheque / postal order for £......... (+ 50p P&P per title) OR please charge my credit card

□ Access / Mastercard □ Visa

CARD NUMBER □□□□ □□□□ □□□□ □□□□
EXPIRY DATE □ □ □□

NAME:...TEL:...

ADDRESS:...

....

Please send orders to : THE O'BRIEN PRESS, 20 VICTORIA ROAD, DUBLIN 6.
Tel : (Dublin) 4923333 Fax: (Dublin) 4922777